BURT FRANKLIN: RESEARCH & SOURCE WORKS SERIES 897
Philosophy Monograph Series 88

AN ESSAY

ON THE

NEW ANALYTIC OF LOGICAL FORMS

AN ESSAY

NEW ANALYTIC OF LOGICAL FORMS

BEING THAT WHICH GAINED THE PRIZE PROPOSED BY SIR WILLIAM
HAMILTON, IN THE YEAR 1846, FOR THE BEST EXPOSITION OF
THE NEW DOCTRINE PROPOUNDED IN HIS LECTURES

WITH

AN HISTORICAL APPENDIX

BY THOMAS SPENCER BAYNES

BURT FRANKLIN
NEW YORK

BC
50
B3
1971

Published by LENOX HILL Pub. & Dist. Co. (Burt Franklin)
235 East 44th St., New York, N.Y. 10017
Originally Published: 1850
Reprinted: 1971
Printed in the U.S.A.

S.B.N.: 8337-01975
Library of Congress Card Catalog No.: 73-168274
Burt Franklin: Research and Source Works Series 897
Philosophy Monograph Series 88

Reprinted from the original edition in the University of
Pennsylvania, Library.

CONTENTS.

PREFACE.

THE following Essay was written exclusively from the notes which I took while attending SIR WILLIAM HAMILTON'S class in 1845-6, that being the only session during which I ever attended his logical course as a student.

It has thus a certain value, though this be but slight,* as evidence that SIR W. HAMILTON then taught his new doctrine so clearly, that it might be readily apprehended in all its essential points by an ordinary student. In order, therefore, that it may not lose any accidental value which it possesses on this account, the Essay is published as it was originally written. I should not, indeed, have felt myself at liberty, even on other grounds, to have altered it. Accordingly, with the single excep-

---

* Were it necessary, abundant evidence might be at once obtained to prove that Sir W. Hamilton taught his new doctrine five years earlier than the above date.

tion of a somewhat fuller statement of the three canons of figure, (pages 67, 68,) it is printed without alteration, as at first given in for competition. A few foot-notes have been added while it was going through the press. These are distinguished from the original notes of the Essay by being placed within brackets. Some historical details, too, touching the doctrine which the Essay expounds, have been given in the form of an Appendix. These details, though presenting little attraction to those who have only a general acquaintance with logical science, will, I hope, be found of some interest to its more advanced students.

The few definitions and canons which occur through the Essay, and which are marked with inverted commas, are given from my notes of the lectures. They are, I believe, substantially correct ; but as the notes are in many places brief and imperfect, I cannot vouch for their verbal accuracy. The requirements originally prescribed for the Essay are reprinted with it, as they to some extent explain the form which it assumed.

Although at the time when the prize was awarded SIR WILLIAM HAMILTON had suggested to me that the Essay was of sufficient general interest for publication, still I naturally felt that, in the event of being printed, it would be more satisfactory, both to the public and to myself, to receive some formal confirmation of this. Indeed, as the Essay is mainly devoted to the exposition of SIR W. HAMILTON'S new doctrine, I should not, for a moment, have entertained the idea of publishing it at all without his express sanction. Accordingly, when I first thought of doing so, I applied to SIR W. HAMILTON for this purpose, and received from him the following note, for the kindness of which, I need scarcely say, I feel personally indebted :—

" EDINBURGH, *9th March*, 1850.

" MY DEAR MR. BAYNES,—So far from having any objection to the publication of your Logical Essay, the intention has my fullest approval. When I first perused that Essay, it seemed to me, not only preeminently entitled to the annual prize for which it was written, but well deserving of the attention of logical readers in general. This I probably expressed to you at the time. And having now obtained all the highest honours in Philosophy proper which our University offers to her Alumni, I am happy to learn that you propose printing that Essay, in its original form, with the addition of relative

matters furnished by your subsequent thought and
reading. I am acquainted with no one who has
more zealously—more unexclusively followed out his
philosophical and, in particular, his logical researches;
your supplement cannot, therefore, fail to be at once
curious and important. I would say, that any information from me is at your service, were I not aware
that you are laudably desirous to limit your additions to your own resources. I shall only request
the annexation of a note, principally for the purpose
of showing in what respect my present views may
differ from those of mine stated by you in the Essay.*
—Believe me," &c.

I have only further to return my best thanks to
Sir W. Hamilton for his constant kindness in facili-
tating my inquiries, giving me free access to his
library for works which I could not otherwise have
obtained, and in various other ways affording me
the benefit of his invaluable counsel and assistance.

THOs. S. BAYNES.

Edinburgh, *May* 23, 1850.

* See Note by Sir William Hamilton, p. 153.

ESSAY ON THE NEW ANALYTIC OF LOGICAL FORMS.

Without wishing to prescribe any definite order, it is required that there should be stated in the Essays :—

1° What Logic *postulates* as a condition of its applicability ?

2° The reasons why common language makes an *ellipsis* of the *expressed quantity*, frequently of the *subject*, and more frequently of the *predicate*, though both have always their quantities in thought.

3° Conversion of propositions on the *common* doctrine.

4° Defects of this.

5° *Figure* and *Mood* of Categorical Syllogism and *Reduction*,— on *common* doctrine. (General Statement.)

6° Defects of this. (General Statement.)

7° The one *Supreme Canon* of Categorical syllogisms.

8° The evolution from this canon of all the *Species* of Syllogism.

9° The evolution from this canon of all the *General Laws* of Categorical Syllogisms.

10° The error of the *Special Laws* for the several Figures of Categorical Syllogisms.

11° *How Many Figures* are there ?

12° What are the *Canons* of the *several Figures?*

13° *How many Moods* are there in *all* the Figures ; showing, in concrete examples, through all the Moods, the *unessential* variation which Figure makes in a Syllogism ?

14° What relation do the figures hold to *Extension* and *Comprehension ?*

15° Why have the *second* and *third* Figures *no determinate major* and *minor premises*, and *two* indifferent *conclusions;* while the *first* Figure has a *determinate major* and *minor premise*, and a *single proximate conclusion ?*

16° What relation do the Figures hold to *Deduction* and *Induction ?*

April 15, 1846.

NEW ANALYTIC OF LOGICAL FORMS.

THE main principle on which the new Analytic of
Logical Forms proceeds is that of a thorough-going
quantification of the predicate. This principle in its
full scientific significance has been totally overlooked
by logicians ; and when noticed at all, has for the
most part been referred to only to be discarded as
useless, if not to be condemned as false.* In conse-

---

* Dico, signum esse addendum subjecto, nunquam prædicato. Si
enim in propositione universali affirmativa signum universale addas
prædicato, falsa erit propositio : ut " omnis homo est omne animal."
Si vero in universali negativa signum universale, itemque particulari,
sive affirmativa fuerit sive negativa, signum particulare addideris
prædicatis, propositiones non quidem falsæ fient, sed tamen efficies
redundantiam et ταυτολογίαν. *Doctrina Propositionum Disputa-
tionibus*, xii. *comprehensa*. à M. Daniele Stahlio. Oxon. 1663. (Dis-
putatio vi. § 16.)

[This is the tradition touching the express quantification of the predicate almost universally prevalent in the Aristotelic schools and
commentaries, as will be more fully shown in the Appendix. The
Regulæ Philosophicæ of Stahl, however, from which it is taken, is an
acute and valuable work, faithful to its title, and containing more
learning and philosophy than could readily, even in the works of his

quence of this omission, logic as a formal science has
received only a one-sided development—has been
deprived of much that is scientifically true—encumbered with much that is scientifically false ; and

time, be found within the same compass. It long maintained a very
high reputation, and was often reprinted, both on the continent and
in this country. The first edition was published in 1635, the second
in 1641, another in 1653. Several others followed, which were reprinted at London and Oxford ; and finally a revised edition appeared
in 1676, with notes by the elder Thomasius, who was the master of
Leibnitz. From having thus ascertained more accurately the dates of
the earlier editions of this work, I can now state with confidence
what I had before surmised, viz., that it contains at least a partial
anticipation of the distinction which was for the first time fully taken
and established in modern philosophy by the Port-Royal logicians,—
the distinction, to wit, in notions of the two wholes or quantities,
the *comprehensive* and the *extensive*. In answer to the question, how
the wider predicate comes to be in its narrower subject ; or, what is
the same thing, how the whole essence of the genus comes to be in
the species ; the author says, " Esse prædicatum in aliquo subjecto
totum seu universaliter potest dupliciter accipi : primo, *intensive* seu
ratione essentiæ, et sic animal totum inest homini, et sic quodvis prædicatum superius inest inferiori : secundo, *extensive*, seu *ratione la-
titudinis* ut hic accipitur, et sic animal non inest totum seu universaliter in homine, quia animal non totum comprehenditur ab ipso,
ita ut extra ipsum non sit." (*Reg. Phil.*, p. 687.) The contrasted
character of these counter quantities, the intensive, as the *quantity
of essence*, the extensive, as the *quantity of extent*, is here given with
even scientific precision. Many of the older logicians say in general,
(after Aristotle,) that in one sense the species is in the genus, and
in another the genus in the species ; but I have not found any statement of this distinction before the time of the Port-Royalists at all
so precise and explicit as that given in the above passage. Daniel
Stahl, beside the *Regulæ*, was the author of a number of other works
on Logic, Metaphysics, and Ethics. He was professor of Philosophy
in the University of Jena, and died in the year 1654, after having
occupied the chair thirty-one years. (*Witteni Memoriæ*, p. 166.)]

throughout its entire history exhibited in a perverted and erroneous form. On the principle of a quantified predicate, however, past evils are corrected, past omissions supplied; and logic receives its highest development in the perfection and simplicity of its form. To exhibit some of the more immediate improvements thus effected by the application of this principle is the design of the following essay. In seeking to accomplish this there will be;—

I. A statement and application of the fundamental postulate of logic, from which application there arises the principle of an expressed quantification of the predicate.

II. The application of this principle (of a quantified predicate) to propositions ; and in particular to the doctrine of their conversion, in which the complexity and incompleteness of the old doctrine will be contrasted with the simplicity and perfection of the new.

III. The influence of this principle on the doctrine of categorical syllogisms, in contributing to effect specially ; the reduction of their general laws to one ; the abolition of their special laws ; and from this new simplicity the amplification of the valid forms of reasoning.

[It may, perhaps, be well to state at the outset that in the following essay, when not otherwise stated, we proceed in the whole commonly recognised by logicians—the whole of Extension ; understanding, however, that by changing the copula in propositions, and accompanying this change by a transposition of the propositions in syllogisms, what is said of the one whole of Extension is equally applicable to the counter whole of Comprehension.]

We proceed then—

I. *To state and apply the fundamental postulate of logic. This postulate is,—" That we be allowed to state in language what is contained in thought."*

The application of this postulate to the subject of a proposition is not denied. Logicians *now* universally allow that the subject has a determinate quantity in thought, and this is accordingly expressed in language. With the subject of a proposition we have here, therefore, nothing to do. It is to the predicate that we have to vindicate an interest in the postulate co-equal with that of the subject.

In order to determine this, we must inquire whether a notion holding the place of predicate in a proposition always has a determinate* quantity in thought.

---

* In order to obviate mistake, we may say that we use the word " *determinate*," in relation to quantity, generically, as including under it *definite* (universal or individual) *and indefinite* (particular). In this sense it is simply opposed to that absence of all expressed quantity which logicians have generally represented by the term *indefinite*. We do not know whether such usage be strictly correct, but adopt it for the sake of convenience.

If it have, then the postulate has an immediate application, and this quantity must be expressed.

In answering this question we shall show—

i. *That the predicate always has a determinate quantity in thought: and* ii., *Explain the reason why this quantity is not generally expressed in common language.*

We proceed to show then—

i. That a notion holding the place of predicate in a proposition always has a determinate quantity in thought.

That this is the case will appear from a little consideration of what a notion is. " A notion or concept"* is defined to be "the cognition or idea of the

---

* [As this term has fallen out of use, it may be necessary to say a word or two in explanation of its recall. It is employed by Sir W. Hamilton to discriminate in conception the *product* from the *process.* The meaning of the term conception, as commonly used, is ambiguous, since it is employed to denote both the *act* of conceiving and the *product* of that act. The correlative term *concept* removes this ambiguity, since it designates exclusively the product, while the term *conception* is restricted to denote the act of conceiving. It need scarcely be added that these terms are here employed according to their true etymological and scientific meaning, to denote the acts and products of the comparative, and not those of the representative faculty.

We said advisedly that this term had " fallen out of use," inasmuch as it was commonly employed by the older English writers on Logic in its precise scientific significance, to express those generalisations represented by common terms, which are the ultimate elements of logical analysis, and with which the first part of logic has mainly to do. Thus Coke, speaking of first and second notions, says—" Those that primarily imposed names intended to name first the things

general attribute or attributes in which a plurality of
objects coincide." This obviously involves the perception of a number of objects—their comparison—
the recognition of their points of similarity—and their
subjective union by this common attribute. The

themselves, as the word *man* is to express primarily the *conceit* which
we form of human nature." Again, " Now the second notions do
not directly and by themselves shadow out unto us the things themselves, nor anything accidental or appendant unto them, but point
out certain intellectual rules whereby we do with all distinctness
and regularity form things, that is the *conceits* of things." (*Art of
Logick*, p. 11.) And again, speaking of the various relations of words,
he says quite explicitly—" The formal is the signification of the word,
and by consequence the relation to the *conceit* of the mind which it
giveth knowledge of." (P. 15.) Fraunce also uses the term continually. Thus, to take a single example in defining an axiom, he
says, " It here signifieth any sentence or proposition whatsoever
wherein one argument, reason, *conceipt*, thing, is so conjoined with,
or severed from another, as that thereby we judge the one eyther to bee
or not to bee, the cause, effect ; whole, part ; generall, speciall ; subject,
adjunct : divers, disparate ; relative, repugnant ; like, unlike ; equall
more or less to the other." (*Lawyer's Logick*, fol. 87.) See another
instance of this use from Fraunce in the quotation given at p. 23
(note). The term is also used by Granger in his " Divine Logick ;"
and, if I remember aright, by Wilson in his " Rule of Reason." It is
to be found, too, employed in the same sense out of logical works, and
is used in this way by writers of authority ; we may specify as examples among others Dr. Henry More, and Sir W. Raleigh. All that
now remains to us of this old use is the restricted sense in which the
word *conceit* is employed—a sense at once so restricted and so established as to unfit it for scientific use. *Concept*, as strictly analo-
gical in form and precise in meaning, is exactly the term we need to
express the simplest products of the comparative faculty ; and, as
we have shown, it already exists in the language. What is necessary,
therefore, in employing it, is not an apology for its introduction, but
simply a vindication of its recall.]

possibility of this process determines the possibility of knowledge to man.   Had he no power of classifying in intellect the confused multitude of objects presented in sense, he must remain for ever destitute of anything worthy of the name of knowledge.   With no clear recognition even of the individual, since comparison and discrimination would be impossible, he must for ever abide amidst the obscurity and vagueness in which knowledge commences—helpless amidst a multiplicity of objects which he could not comprehend—bewildered by a confusion which there was no possibility of recalling to order.   The earliest effort of the mind is accordingly directed to extricate itself from this confusion ; and this determines the exercise of the comparative faculty, and the formation of concepts or notions.

Amidst the multitude of confused objects presented to the mind in perception, some are found to affect us similarly in certain respects.   These objects the mind considers ; by comparison it recognises their resembling qualities ; by attention these are exclusively considered, since the concentration of the mind on those qualities in which objects coincide involves of necessity its abstraction from those in which they are severally dissimilar.   These various objects, since the resembling attributes which they possess in common cannot, when considered alone, be discriminated, are, in this restricted point of view, considered as one.   In other words, the mind grasps into unity a multitude of objects severally distinct by a common point of identity. On this unity thus formed it sets the seal of a name, that it may be enabled ever afterwards at once to discriminate the various objects of its knowledge, commodiously refer each to its own class, and thus be saved the endless labour of enumerating all the particulars by which objects are individually discriminated. A notion is thus a purely ideal or subjective whole, which the mind from the limitation of its powers is necessitated to form, in order to classify in thought and discriminate in language the various objects of its knowledge.

This being the case, it is obvious that a concept or notion can afford only a partial knowledge, and has only a relative existence. It can afford only a partial knowledge, since it embraces some only of the many marks by which an object is known. It has only a relative existence, since this knowledge is not given absolutely, but only in connexion with some one of the objects to which the concept is related. For a notion, though potentially applicable to all the objects which it contains, can only be truly known on occasion of its being actually applied to some one of these objects. This is at once the test and the evidence of its relative character. And this being its character, it is obviously altogether dependent on the objects from which it is formed. A notion has thus, in its totality, a purely subjective existence, destitute of any objective reality. Being what it is

—an ideal whole only by relation to the objects whose resembling part it embraces—it is obvious, as we have said, that it can pretend to no independent existence, much less to any independent knowledge. Its existence entirely depends on that of the objects from whence it is derived, and to each of which it is linked by the common resembling attribute which it embraces. Destroy the objects, you destroy the resembling attributes in each ; and destroying the resembling parts, you annihilate the whole which they together constituted. As, however, a concept has only a subjective being, existence and knowledge are here identical. If no qualities be discriminated in objects as similar, we have no knowledge of a concept—no concept exists. If we cannot assign an object to any class—cannot say it does or does not belong to any notion, we do not comprehend it. We think an object (recognise to be what it is) only as we think it under some notion or concept.

This being premised with regard to notions in general, it will be seen, that when we bring an object under a notion, *i.e.*, when we predicate of it that it belongs to such a class, we must know that it occupies a certain place in that class. For if we were uncertain what place the individual object occupied in the class, or whether it occupied any place at all, we should not know the class, and could not, therefore, bring any object under it;—*e.g.*, If I do not know whether *rose* comes under the concept *flower*

—whether it is equal to some part, or the whole, or superior to it—I do not know the class *flower*, and cannot, of course, predicate flower of rose ; in other words, I cannot bring *rose* under the concept *flower*, since I do not know what the concept means, what it contains, and what it does not. This is clear ; for as we have just explained—since a notion, as a factitious unity in thought, is absolutely worthless, and, indeed, not cognisable, out of relation to the individual objects, the aggregate of whose resembling qualities it constitutes ; and since an object is truly known only as it is thought through or under a notion, it follows, that comprehension, in such a case, would be impossible. If, therefore, we understand the object at all, we must fix, in thought, the sphere which it occupies under the class to which, in predication, we have assigned it. In other words—if we comprehend what we utter, *every notion holding the place of predicate in a proposition must have a determinate quantity in thought.*

This, indeed, is always involved in predication. For predication is nothing more or less than the expression of the relation of quantity in which a notion stands to an individual, or two notions to each other. If this relation were indeterminate— if we were uncertain whether it was of part, or whole, or none—there could be no predication. The very fact of predication is thus always evidence that the predicate notion holds a relation of determinate

quantity to the subject. In other words, we think
only as we think under some determinate quantity ;
for all thought is comparison of less and more, of
part and whole. All predication is but the utterance
of thought. All predication must, therefore, have a
determinate quantity.

*Since, therefore, the quantity always exists in
thought, the postulate applies; that is, in logic the
quantity must be expressed, on demand, in language.*

It only remains to remark here, that this quantity
of the predicate notion, always determinate, will be
definite, (universal or individual,) or *indefinite*, (particular,) as the subject notion is greater, equal to, or
less than the predicate. If the subject notion be
less, we attribute to it a part only of the predicate—
say it is some part, but not the whole, which that
notion comprises, *e.g.*, " *all man is some mortal.*" If
the subject be equal to the predicate, we attribute
the whole notion to it, *e.g.*, " *all man is all rational.*"
If the subject be greater, we attribute the whole predicate to it, as a part only of its extension, *e.g.*,
" *some mortal is all man.*"

Logicians who have occasionally touched upon the
quantification of the predicate, seem for the most
part to have conceived the possibility of its express
quantification only universally ;* and because this

---

* Notandum, signum universalitatis non esse apponendum prædicato, sed tantum subjecto ; rectè enim dicitur, " *omnis homo est
animal;*" sed non rectè dicitur, " *omnis homo est omne animal.*"

cannot be done in a great number of cases—in all those cases, indeed, in which an individual is brought under a concept, or a species under a genus, (as we cannot say, "all man is all mortal,")—since this cannot be done, to have lightly thereupon thrown aside the whole doctrine as of no avail. It is, however, clear, from the nature of a notion as a whole made up of the like characters in a number of objects which thus stand to it in the relation of parts, that we are quite as much at liberty to say of one of these objects, that it forms a part of the notion, as we are to say of all the objects together, that they constitute the whole.*   We may, therefore, and in

---

Verum duæ limitationes adhiberi possunt: Prima, ut intelligatur de universalibus affirmatis non autem de negatis ; recte enim dicitur "*omnis homo est nullus asinus,*" "*nullus asinus est omnis homo :*" Secunda, ut signum universalitatis immediatè ponatur ante prædicatum ; nam si apponatur tantùm adjuncto prædicati, enunciatio non erit falsa, ut "*visus percipit omnem colorem,*" "*Christus curabat omnem morbum,*" &c. Quia adjunctum ejusmodi poterit fieri subjectum, mutando verbum activum in passivum hoc pacto, "*omnis color percipitur a visu.*"   *Davidis Derodonis Logica Restituta.* Geneva, 1659.   (Page 573.)

On the catholic doctrine held by logicians touching the quantification of the predicate, see the Appendix.

* [The older logicians laid down many rules which were often useless, sometimes false, and at best of only partial and limited application, about what they termed the regular and irregular order of predication—the natural or unnatural, direct or indirect, consecution of the terms in a proposition. Natural, or regular, or direct predication (*predicatio naturalis, directa, ordinata*) they held to be that in which the genus is predicated of the species, the species of the individual, the attribute of its subject, and in general the exten-

fact we must continually quantify the predicate particularly.

sive whole of its part ; and in which, therefore, the subject notion was always of less extent than the predicate notion. Unnatural, indirect or irregular predication (*predicatio non naturalis, indirecta, inordinata*) was the reverse of this, that, to wit, in which the species was predicated of the genus, the subject of its attribute, and in general the extensive part of its whole.

Language is, however, but the instrument of thought ; and its natural order in the last resort must ever be that in which it best expresses the thought of which it is the vehicle. What this order shall be will thus in great measure be determined by the feeling and purpose of the speaker. If he have a special interest in any particular term, or wishes in any way to make it emphatic, it will occupy the more prominent and important place in the proposition. The order in such a case will be that of interest and emphasis, and this surely is as natural an arrangement as any other. Accordingly, if I wish to direct particular attention to the genus, it may stand first in the proposition, and the species follow as its predicate. Thus, for example, if referring to the Scaligers I were to say, " An acute philosopher was the father, an erudite philologer the son," there would be nothing unnatural in this, for by such an arrangement of the terms, I simply direct special attention to the different departments of science in which they respectively excelled. So, again, in the line of the poet, " The proper study of mankind is man ;" and in a number of other examples that will readily suggest themselves. With equal justice, if I wish to make the species (or genus) emphatic, I may predicate the individual of it, *e.g.*, in the expressions, " A philosopher, indeed, was Socrates ;" " The poet of all time is Shakspeare ;" there is nothing unnatural, but attention is appropriately directed to the high type of poetic and philosophic character which respectively belonged to these great men.

It is no valid objection to this form of predication to say, that in all such cases we do in reality so restrict the genus or species, that they become convertible with the species or individual severally predicated of them ; for this objection lies equally against all predication whatever. Thus, in what is termed the regular form, the genus is never

We proceed then—

ii. To explain why the quantity of the predicate is not expressed in common language.

We have already explained the nature of a con-

taken in the whole of its extent, but only in so much of it as is oc-cupied by the species of which it is predicated, *e.g.*, when we say, " All man is animal," we do not of course mean *all* animal, but simply that *part* of animal which is convertible with man, or as is sometimes more explicitly stated, " Man is an (one) animal," or, (if referring to the race,) " a species of animal."

So, again, in relation to the second division of what is called un-natural predication—that in which the subject is predicated of its attribute—if we wish specially to signalise the attribute that will naturally stand first, *e.g.*, in the exclamation, " Great is Diana of the Ephesians," the greatness of Diana is far more emphatically marked than it would be if the terms were reversed. So, again, in the line, " The fairest of her daughters, Eve," it is to the beauty of Eve that special attention is directed.

It may be at once conceded to the logicians, that what they have termed the natural or direct order, is the more common, inasmuch as the concrete terms of a proposition are generally of greater interest than the abstract ones ; but it is unjust to speak of any other order of predication as unnatural or unlawful, while it is quite obvious that, logically considered, either order of consecution in the terms of a proposition is equally valid, for we may indifferently predicate a part of the genus of the whole species, or the whole species of a part of the genus. This liberty, indeed, is not denied, though it is generally, nevertheless, even by late writers, allowed as an exception rather than as a rule. Thus Gassendi, after giving the rule that the species cannot be predicated of the genus, says, in mitigation of its force— " Additur nihilominus, *nisi generi limitatio adhibeatur ;* dicere enim possumus, ut jam ante insinuatum est, *aliquod animal est homo ; certus quidam color est candor ; una quæpiam virtus est justitia.* Efficitur nempe, ut particulis hujusmodi limitantibus genus veluti contrahatur, neque amplius pateat, quam species ; ac proinde ut species de eo enunciari, fierive illius attributum reciproce possit." (*Logica.* Oxon. 1718, p. 367.)]

cept—that it is a factitious whole obtained from a
number of individual objects, each of which, therefore, occupies a certain part of the whole concept.
We have also shown, that this relation of quantity is
always present to the mind, when a concept and an
individual (or a part and whole of any kind) are
thought together as subject and predicate.   Though
always thus contained in thought, this quantity is,
however, rarely expressed in ordinary language.
The name in which the totality of attribute embraced by the concept is fixed, is usually applied
to any one of its individual objects, without any
particle of quantification.   The explanation of this
omission is to be found in the end which common language seeks.   The end which it proposes
to itself is the clear utterance of meaning ; it seeks
to render at once intelligible, by its signs, *the thing
signified.*   As a vehicle for the conveyance of thought,
ordinary language is mainly concerned about *what is
thought*—not the *manner of thinking it.*   In other
and more technical terms, it is primarily engaged
with the *matter of thought,* and only considers the
form incidentally, and as a mean to an end.   Whatever, therefore, is not really necessary to the clear
comprehension of what is contained in thought, is
usually elided in expression.   Thus common language abounds with abbreviations and elliptical
forms of expression.   The expression of those phases
of thought and feeling which arise in conjunctions of

circumstances which are frequent and familiar, are almost always and conveniently of this description, *e.g.,*—we meet a friend and say, " *good morning.*" What is intended here ? A cordial greeting and the expression of friendly feeling. This, however, is not expressed in terms, but the elliptical form above is understood to represent, " I wish you a good morning." So also in " farewell," and a multitude of other cases which might be adduced. In fact, so that what is meant by it be at once clearly intelligible, an expression, however elliptical, is true and valid for all the purposes of ordinary language. Thus, to facilitate the communication of thought, not only are words omitted, but the steps of the reasoning process itself are for the most part abbreviated. Common language almost invariably makes an ellipsis of one step of this process. For since the reasoning process is the same in all men—being governed by laws necessary and universal—the mind at once and intuitively supplies the omitted step, and the process is complete. This principle, too, affords the true explanation why, in common language, the overt quantification of the predicate is neglected. It is not necessary for the clear comprehension of a proposition that the predicate be quantified in terms. And the reason why this is not necessary is to be found in the universality of generalisation or the formation of concepts, and the sameness of the process in all men. All men must generalise, for the

necessity which determines this process exists in all.
All men must generalise alike, for the faculties which
accomplish it are the same in all.   In order to comprehend the many objects by which he is surrounded,
he must reduce them to order.   To accomplish this,
he classifies or groups into unity a number of objects
which affect him in the same manner.   But as the
same objects affect all men in the same manner, it
follows, that where the same term exists to express
the same mental modification, this term may and
will be applied to all the individual objects which
determine such similar impressions.

As all men, therefore, know what is meant by a
general term,—that it is a name equally applicable to
all and each of the individual objects which it embraces, when one of these objects is brought under
it ; that is to say, when it is predicated of this object
that it forms a part of the notion which the general
term expresses, it is not absolutely necessary overtly
to declare that it forms only some part ; for as it is
universally known that the concept is of far wider
extension, the quantity is immediately supplied in
thought, and no mistake arises.   Thus, when we say,
" *Every horse is an animal*"—" *All men are mortal,*"
it is not necessary to say that there are other animals besides horses, or to guard explicitly against
the conclusion that man alone is mortal ; for as the
extension of the general terms is understood by all,
every one knows at once, by a reference to the matter

of the thought, that in each case the predicate is affirmed of its subject only in *some part* of its extension, not in the whole.

Since, therefore, it is not necessary, for the clear understanding of a proposition, that the predicate notion be expressly quantified, and as the continual repetition of it would be wearisome, the quantification is usually omitted ; in other words, *since it is not necessary for the purposes which ordinary language seeks to accomplish, the quantity of the predicate, though always contained in thought, is usually elided in expression.*

All this, however, becomes widely different when in the progress of reflective inquiry a science arises, which seeks, as its express aim, to accomplish a full and final analysis *of the form of thought*. It will be the office of such a science to supply for its own purposes the omissions of common language—to restore whatever of the form of thought may have fallen out of expression in ordinary parlance. The procedure of logic and that of common language are thus different, and to some extent opposed ; the former recalling to expression as of scientific value what the latter had thrown aside as of no account. The different nature of their procedure is, as we have hinted, determined by the different nature of the ends which they respectively seek to accomplish. Common language, as we have seen, seeks as its end to exhibit with *clearness the matter of thought*. Whatever does not contribute to this is thrown aside as worthless. Logic, on the other hand, seeks as its end *to exhibit with exactness the form of thought.* Whatever contributes to this is retained as of scientific value. All the elements which the analysis of the form of thought furnishes must be brought out to view, and explicitly considered. Whatever does not belong to the form of thought must be cast aside as without the province of the science. We have seen, that in thought the predicate notion of a proposition is always of a given quantity. This quantity is not expressed in common language ; because, by a knowledge of, and reference to, the matter of thought, the omission is at once supplied. This procedure is, however, of course incompetent to logic. As a formal science, it knows nothing of the matter of thought ; it makes no elisions ; it can understand nothing ; it can supply nothing ; it can only recognise and deal scientifically with what is given formally. If, therefore, the predicate has always a certain quantity in thought, (and we have shown it has,) that quantity must be expressed before it can be logically taken into account, and its significance investigated. The recognition of the expressed quantity of the predicate is then as imperative in logic as the neglect of such recognition is convenient in common language ; for it is plain that, unless all the elements furnished by analysis be received and considered in their relative influence and importance, the science cannot pretend to completeness. Logic, in common with all sciences, seeks perfection ; but, as a formal science, it can only realise scientific perfection as it attains to formal exactness. The condition of its formal exactness is, that its analysis of the form of thought be exhaustive and complete. As soon as this is the case, synthesis may commence, and the science will emerge in its full beauty and true perfection.

This explains how it is that logic has remained so imperfect and deformed in the hands of all previous logicians. They were, in the main, right as far as they went ; but they did not go far enough. Their investigation of the form of thought was arrested before it had attained the necessary completeness. Proceeding in their analysis, they correctly recalled to expression what common language had omitted in the reasoning process, and exhibited the three steps of that process in their formal order and completeness. Still continuing their analysis, they proceeded to investigate the properties of a proposition in order to determine its scientific capabilities. Here they discovered that the subject has always a certain quantity in thought. This quantity, in conformity with the necessities of their science, they accordingly expressed, and turned to scientific account. But here their analysis was stopped, just at the very point the investigation of which would have conferred upon their science the completeness which it lacked ;

and, as the natural result of a defective analysis, logic, as a science, has always remained incomplete. Had logicians proceeded further, they would have discovered that a determinate quantity always belongs, not only to the subject of a proposition, but also to the predicate ; that the recognition of this quantity in logic affords an important principle, the true application of which would relieve it of its many inconsistencies, and confer upon it scientific perfection. It will be our business presently to inquire into some of the improvements thus effected.

To recapitulate, then :—We have seen, from the nature of a notion in general, and of a predicate notion in particular, that it always has a determinate quantity in thought. We have thus vindicated to it an interest in the fundamental postulate of logic. And from the application of that postulate there has emerged the principle—*That the quantity of the predicate notion of a proposition be explicitly noted in logic.*

We proceed now to show—

II.—*The application of this principle to propositions, and in particular to the doctrine of their conversion.*

A proposition is defined to be " the expression in language of the relation of congruence or confliction, in which two notions, two individuals, or an individual and a notion, (in a word, two terms,) are recognised, when compared together, to stand to each other." *

This being the nature of a proposition, it is evident that it involves a plurality of ideas,† thought together in mutual relation and dependence; since it is only by being viewed in relation as subject and predicate, determining and determined, that a plurality of thoughts can be reduced to a mental oneness, and recognised together in the same individual act of consciousness.

The terms of a proposition are thus always related, and this relation constitutes their scientific significance. To investigate this relation fully, and determine it exactly, is the office of logical analysis. As a proposition is the expression of the relation of congruence or confliction between two thoughts, it is surely of the highest importance—in fact, a condition of its intelligible existence—that the amount of this agreement or difference be known and stated. This can only be done by ascertaining the quantity of both the terms, and thus determining the space of each in relation to the other. Until this be done, the properties of a proposition have not been fully analysed ; its scientific capabilities cannot be fully determined. The quantity of the terms in relation

* "*Judicium* est comparatio ideæ cum idea ; *propositio* est judicium terminis expressum."—*Ploucquet.*

† Using the term "idea" generically, to include the products of sense, imagination, and intellect.

to each other is thus the most important aspect in which a proposition can be considered ; but though thus the most important relation, it is one in the analysis of which logicians in general seem to have been more than commonly unsuccessful.   In opposition to the obvious importance and necessity of determining the quantity of the terms in a proposition, they have introduced into logic a class of propositions distinguished by the absence of all quantity ;* and this, too,

* [The class of propositions distinguished by the absence of all expressed quantity, and termed by logicians *indefinite*, (more properly *indesignate*,) affords another curious illustration of how completely the force of authority has in logic prevailed over the most obvious and elementary necessities of the science.   Introduced originally by Aristotle, and subsequently reproduced by Boëthius, these propositions have continued to occupy a place in the science, and to be discriminated as a separate class, under the division of quantity.   In the absence of all expressed quantity, however, it was very difficult to turn them to any logical account.   Some kind of quantity was necessary for this purpose ; but the only way in which they could be quantified with any certainty was *particularly*, according to the caution of Apuleius, who says, referring to the division of propositions under the head of quantity, " Aliæ indefinitæ, ut *animal spirat*, non enim definit utrum omne, an aliquod.   Sed tamen pro particulari semper valet.   Quia tutius est id ex incerto accipere quod minus est."   (*De Syllogismo Categorico.   Apuleii Opera.* Lugd., 1600, p. 415.)

Subsequently, however, as stated in the text, rules for determining this quantity were laid down, derived from the object-matter of the propositions themselves.   By Ramus, indeed, and some of his followers, indefinites, it would seem, were altogether rejected as of no logical account.   His English representative, Fraunce, (I have not Ramus' own works at hand,) says, referring to the indefinite proposition, " But Ramus expelleth that uncertaine and indefinite axiom ; for every conceipt of the mind is determinatly eyther generall or

in opposition to the fundamental postulates of their science :—that in order to deal with a proposition we must know what it means—*i.e.*, understand the quantity of its subject and predicate—and that we be

speciall, and speciall eyther particular or singular." (*Lawyer's Logike*, fol. 92.)

They continued, nevertheless, to be currently received, and a later English writer but reflects this common acceptance when he makes them the matter of special legislation. " The canons hereof," says Coke, speaking of this class, " are two." He then gives the following, which are, however, but translations and abridgments from Keckermann :—

" 1. The chief force and use of indefinites is in propositions of the idea : that is in such as where the universal subject is taken absolutely, as—the Lord's Supper is a sacrament ; man is the noblest creature ; the soul of man is immortal, &c.

" 2. There is also a use of indefinites to signifie that the consequent is in the antecedent, for the most part, though not always, ὡς ἐπὶ τὸ πολύ. As, the *Cretians* be lyars ; mothers are too much cockerers of their children," &c. (*Art of Logick*, p. 106.)

A recent British writer, however, sees far more clearly into their true logical character and relation, and says of them, (referring to the rules which are given for their reduction,) with far more scientific than historic truth, " By reduction here is to be understood that logicians recognise no indefinite propositions, and that if an indefinite occur, they require it to be expressed in a definite form. Indefinite propositions are noticed that the logician should be on his guard against them, and not because they are legitimate, or of any legitimate class." (*Thynne's Compendium of Logic*. Dublin, 1827, p. 47.)

This is far from being historically true, and if it were, it would not avail to defend the position which indefinites occupy ; for the principle of their reduction is as extra-logical as are the propositions to be reduced. In the statement, that they are not recognised in logic as a separate class, this author has at once overrated the acuteness of his predecessors, and underrated his own ; for it is only within a comparatively short period that their logical position has been seri-

allowed to express all that is understood. As an antidote to the disorders thus introduced into their science, they have had recourse to an extra-logical remedy ; that is to say, they have laid down a number of rules for determining the quantity of these unquantified propositions, founded on the object-matter of these propositions themselves, according as this matter is possible or impossible, necessary or contingent. In so doing they have, implicitly at least, destroyed their science ; for if logic be competent to this discrimination, it can no longer vindicate to itself the character of a special science, but must become co-extensive with the whole domain of human knowledge. They have thus also destroyed the possibility of its thorough-going application, since they have tacitly laid down, as a preliminary to such application, the impossible condition that we should

ously called in question. They are, however, as need scarcely now be stated, to be rejected from logic as utterly unscientific in their character. They belong, indeed, to the same confusion of the accidental with the essential, through which the enthymeme was discriminated as a separate form of reasoning. In both the mere *contingencies of speech* are identified with the *necessities of thought;* and the *accidents of expression* are received and incorporated with the science as valid *elements of form.* Science, however, is no longer worthy of the name when it accepts and incorporates, without examination, the rude materials which it is its office to elaborate ; and places among its elements the confused wholes, which a more searching analysis would have decomposed into their constituent parts. This is precisely what has happened in relation to the indefinite proposition and the enthymeme ; and accordingly, by a truer scientific analysis, they are finally rejected from logic.]

know all that is possible and all that is impossible, all that is contingent and all that is necessary. To say nothing of its logical inconsistency,—this being impossible is, as a scientific demand, absurd.

Logicians have not, however, of course left propositions generally in this unquantified state, or their science would have remained hopelessly crippled. They proceeded, as we have already said, to consider the quantity of propositions ; but here their inconsistency still attends them, and they are destined to be again unsuccessful. For in their analysis, as we have seen, they have only considered the subject, and determined its quantity, while that of the predicate, which it was equally necessary to determine, as being of equal scientific value, is altogether neglected. The proximate influence of this omission in introducing complexity and inconsistency into the science will be seen in the common doctrine of conversion ; while some of its remoter consequences will be hereafter signalised. It may be well to premise here that we speak of categorical propositions throughout. We go on, then, to notice *the conversion of propositions on the common doctrine.* When the subject and predicate of a proposition change places, the proposition is said *to be converted.*

This conversion is threefold.

1. *Simple conversion.*—This takes place when the terms are simply transposed, without any change of quantity or quality in the proposition. This is com-

petent in universal negative and particular affirmative propositions ; *e.g.*,—

> No man is a stone. Therefore,
> No stone is a man.
> Some man is a tinker. Therefore,
> Some tinker is a man.

2. *Conversion per accidens.*—This takes place when the quality of the two propositions remains the same; but the quantity is altered, the predicate in the one being limited on becoming the subject of the other. This holds true in universal propositions, both affirmative and negative ;* *e.g.*,—

> All violets are flowers. Therefore,
> Some flowers are violets.

---

* [This is the statement of Peter Hispanus, and it has been repeated by Derodon and some others among the later logicians. The application of this species of conversion to universal negatives is, however, altogether useless, as they are converted simply, and thus retain their universality after conversion. It is, moreover, incompetent, inasmuch as, in such a process, an inference of subordination is involved.

By the majority of logical writers it is therefore applied exclusively and formally to universal affirmative propositions. As so applied, however, the name which it bears is unsuitable, since it no longer truly designates the nature of the process which it is employed to express. Taken in this exclusive application, *restrictive* or *attenuate* conversion (the name given to it by Granger) would be much better.

It is worth while noticing, that the logicians in general do not seem to be at all aware by whom this term, *per accidens*, as applied to conversion, was introduced, or what was the kind of process which it was originally employed to denote. None refer to its authorship, while few attempt any explanation of its meaning ; and the few who do are for the most part incorrect. Isenach, whose " *Epitome Dia-*

3. *Conversion by contraposition.**—This takes place when the quality of the propositions remains unaffected ; but the terms are changed into what is called by logicians infinite, but more appropriately

lecticæ" was published about the year 1510, says, in explanation, that this species of conversion was called *per accidens*, because one of the accidents of the proposition (quantity, to wit) was changed. Keckermann gives a somewhat different and longer account of it. He says, that this kind of conversion is called *per accidens*, because the converted is not *immediately* inferred from the converse, but only *mediately* through the intervention of another proposition ; *e.g.*, from the proposition " all man is animal," it is not *immediately* inferred that " some animal is man," but rather that " some man is animal ;" and as this can be converted simply, it follows that " some animal is man." (*Systema Logicæ.* Francof, 1628, p. 348.) While a recent Oxford writer gives the following not very intelligible explanation :— " Per accidens—putting in the place of the subject the quality, whether proprium or accident, which the predicate implies. By the old logicians the proprium is constantly called accidens proprium." (*Moberly's Lectures on Logic.* Oxford, 1848, p. 85.) It is difficult to see how this statement (even supposing it to be just as far as it goes) can be accepted as a full account of the matter,—inasmuch as it can at best only apply to those cases in which the predicate is the property or accident of the subject, and by no means to the generic latitude of possible predication to which the conversion extends. Ploucquet is the only one among modern logicians, so far as my knowledge extends, who seems to have understood the sense in which it was originally employed, and who has accordingly given the true explanation of the term. He says, explaining the significance of the letter P (per accidens) in the mnemonic verses, " Notat universalem in particularem, et particularem in universalem esse convertendam, id quod fit *per accidens*, ex natura *materiæ*." (*Fundamenta Phil. Spec.* Tubingæ, 1758, p. 45.) This is the true explanation of the term, and of the process which it originally designated, as employed

---

* Some logical writers, it appears, have rejected this species as of no logical value.—*Crackanthorpe*, Book iii. chap. 10.

indefinite, by the addition of negative particles ; that is to say, when in the converted proposition, instead of the subject and predicate simply, the contradictory of each is found ; *e.g.*,—

> Every man is mortal.   Therefore,
> Everything which is not mortal is not man.

by Boëthius,* who was the author of this species of conversion, name, and thing. This term was employed by him to denote the conversion of the universal into the particular, and the particular into the universal, from the *accident of the matter* of the proposition. He says, " Harum (propositionum) igitur, particularis affirmatio, particulariter quidem sibi ipsa convertitur, universali autem affirmationi *per accidens,* et rursus universalis negatio, loco principe sui recepit conversionem, ad particularem vero negationem *per accidens* converti potest. Nec vero negationis particularis ad seipsam principaliter stabilis ac firma conversio est, sed negationi universali secundo loco atque accidentaliter." *Introductio ad Syllogismos.* (*Opera, Basil.* 1546, p. 575.)

But the *formal* conversion, (to be carefully distinguished from the *material* conversion of Boëthius,) which the term was subsequently and exclusively employed to denote, had been discriminated long before the time of Boëthius. It was expressly taken by Aristotle, and called by him *partial* or *particular* conversion, (ἀντιστροφὴ ἐν μέρει.) *Anal. Pr.* i. c. 2, § 1.) It was subsequently also signalized by Apuleius under the name of *reflex* conversion. His words are, " Universalis autem dedicativa et ipsa quidem non est conversibilis, sed particulariter tamen potest converti : ut cum sit *omnis homo animal,* non potest ita converti, ut sit *omne animal homo ;* sed particulariter potest, *quoddam animal homo.* Verum hoc in simplici conversione, quæ in conclusionum illationibus *reflexio* nominatur." (*Opera Omnia,* Lugd., 1600, p. 419.)

It may seem useless to have dwelt so long on this kind of conversion in the very act of abolishing it ; but that it is dead is no reason whatever why so venerable a member of the ancient system should not receive decent burial.]

---

* For the reference to Boëthius I am indebted to Sir W. Hamilton.

This holds true in universal affirmative and particular negative propositions. The rules* governing conversion are given by different logicians with numerical differences; in substance, however, they are much the same. But as the enumeration would be tedious, and the nature of the process in its different species is evident from the statement of each, we shall not repeat them here.

We might remark on this process generally, that it is, for the most part, logically incompetent; since in the second species we interpolate a quantity not formally given, and in the third create an entirely new proposition by new terms.

But we pass on to remark, specially, *that the whole doctrine of conversion, as commonly understood, is on the principle of the new analytic false and useless.*

This inconsistent and cumbrous doctrine resulted, as we have said, from a false analysis by logicians of the elements with which they had to deal. The whole doctrine is founded upon the relation of quantity between the subject and predicate in a proposition; but if a principal element of that relation be left out, the doctrine will of course be defective. Logicians stand chargeable with this neglect. They commenced to recompose their system before, by thorough decomposition, they had obtained all the elements requisite

---

* *Crackanthorpe* gives five, *Wallis* six, another British writer twelve.—*The Port-Royal* three, reduced to two.

for that purpose ; and to remedy the deficiencies
thus occasioned, they have had recourse to the com-
plicated process briefly stated above ;—thus, with
labour and difficulty—and even then imperfectly—by
a complex process, and a number of particular rules,
effecting that which a simple proximate principle of
their science would, if recognised, have spontaneously
and perfectly accomplished. As this confusion and
complexity has arisen from a faulty analysis, so a
perfect analysis at once introduces order and simplicity.   A full decomposition of the elements contained
in thought discovers that the predicate is always of
a given quantity in relation to the subject ; that this
is known and recognised as the condition of predication. It thus reveals that the relation between the
terms of a proposition is one not only of similarity,
but of *identity ;* that the subject and predicate of a
proposition, when the relation of each to the other is
recognised, and both are quantified, are always necessarily simply convertible ; that the terms of a proposition, in short, are of an absolute equality, and all
predication an equation of subject and predicate.
Quantify the predicate, and two notions of different
extension are at once brought into equality ; the
sphere of an individual object in a notion is marked
out, and that sphere becomes absolutely convertible
with the object ; *e.g.,*—

> All man is some animal.
> Some animal is all man.

> Some men are all philosophers.
> All philosophers are some men.
>
> Boëthius is some Roman.
> Some Roman is Boëthius.

Thus, on the principle of the new analytic the whole doctrine of ordinary conversion, with its complex species and its manifold rules, passes away, and the whole process becomes as practically simple as it is scientifically complete. The terms of a proposition are exhibited in their true relation, and that relation reduces all the species of conversion to one—*that of simple conversion.* Thus, in the words of an acute writer, whose apt statement in relation to this doctrine is true in a far wider application than he designed it—to the whole and not to a part alone of the doctrine of conversion. " Omnes conversionum leges pendent à cohæsione, vel potius ab identitate subjecti et attributi : quod si enim subjectum conjungitur et *identificatur* ut aiunt, cum attributo, necesse est pariter attributum *uniri* et *identificari* cum subjecto." *

We proceed to consider—

III. *The influence of this principle on the doctrine of categorical syllogisms, in contributing to effect,* 1°, *the reduction of their general laws to one ;* 2°, *the*

---

* " *Philosophia Burgundica,*" 1678, tom. i.　Institutiones Logicæ. Sect. Secunda, cap. 2.　(By Du Hamel.)

abolition of their special laws: and from this new
simplicity the amplification of the valid forms of rea-
soning.

We premise a word or two on the nature of a
syllogism in general, and of a categorical syllogism
in particular.

" A syllogism is the product of that act of mediate
comparison, by which we recognise that two notions
stand to each other in the relation of whole and
part, through the recognition that these notions
severally stand in the same relation to a third."

A syllogism or reasoning is thus like a concept and
a judgment the product of the comparative faculty—
the comparison of part and whole.   This indeed is
the characteristic of all reasoning—alike of the simple
syllogism and of the most lengthy and profound argument. All reasoning is but the comparison and determination of wholes and parts. As in concepts various
attributes, in judgments various thoughts, are compared in order to determine the relation of part and
whole subsisting between them; so in reasoning two
notions are compared together with a third in order
to determine their connexion with each other—the
only difference being the higher complexity which
in this case the act of comparison assumes. A reasoning thus *differs* from a judgment in the superior
complexity of the act, in being an immediate act of
comparison in which two notions, whose relation

to each other is unknown, are compared together through a third, whose connexion with both is recognised. But it *agrees* with a judgment in being an undivided act of mind ; for as the connexion of part and whole between two notions, enounced by a reasoning, is determined by the recognition of their mutual relation to a third ; and as relatives are only recognised together, it follows that it is an undivided act of consciousness.* A syllogism indeed forms as truly a mental whole as a concept, though each is capable of being subsequently analysed for scientific purposes into its constituent elements. On being subjected to such analysis, every true syllogism or reasoning is found to contain three, and no more than three, propositions, each of which has three, and only three, terms. There will be three propositions, since the two notions, touching whose relation the mind is in doubt, are both compared with another whose relation to each is manifest. This affords two propositions, in one of which the third notion is a contained part in relation to one of the doubtful notions ; and in the other a containing whole in relation to the other doubtful notion. And there is of necessity the conclusion in which the doubt is dispelled, and the relation of the two notions themselves determined. This process is in every valid syllogism determined by a law of thought, and the connexion is thus one

* Hic modus (per syllogismum) ratiocinandi est ex simplissimis, et intuitivè uno actu mentis perspicitur.—*Ploucquet*.

of absolute necessity.   There will, it is obvious, be as many valid kinds of syllogism as there are different laws of thought on which they may be respectively founded.

A categorical syllogism is one in whose major premise the relation of the terms is simple ; whose procedure is determined and whose conclusion is necessitated by the laws of identity and contradiction.

Having premised thus much about syllogisms in general, and categorical syllogisms in particular, we shall proceed—

i. *To state with brevity the common doctrine of syllogistic figure, mood, and reduction; and then generally some of the defects by which it is characterised.*

And,

ii. *To state the one supreme canon of the new analytic, which potentially contains the whole doctrine of categorical syllogisms, and then proceed to develop from it some parts of that doctrine.*

We proceed then—

i. *To state the common doctrine of syllogistic figure, mood, and reduction.*

FIGURE.—What is commonly termed by logicians syllogistic figure arises from the relation of the middle term as subject or predicate to the extremes.   The four possible varieties of position which the middle

term may occupy in the premises thus determine
four syllogistic figures.

In the *first figure* the middle term is the subject of
the major premise, and the predicate of the minor ;
e.g.,—

> All rational is risible.
> All man is rational.
> Therefore—All man is risible.

The laws of this figure are—

1. That the subsumption* be affirmative.

---

* [These words sumption and subsumption are new, and may therefore require a few words of explanation if not of defence. They are
introduced and employed by Sir William Hamilton to express the
two first propositions of a syllogism, instead of the common designa-
tions major and minor premise.

We much need apt terms by which to express these members of
the syllogism, and for the creation of new or introduction of foreign
words in such a relation, may certainly urge the first part of the plea
of Lucretius, "propter egestatem linguæ," if we cannot go on to add
with him, " et rerum novitatem." The members to be named are
old enough, but they still have never received precise and discriminative epithets, at least in our logical terminology. The terms major
and minor premise are objectionable, if for no other reason, from the
confusion of terms with propositions likely enough to arise from the
omission of the second member of the term, and the consequent indiscriminate use in hasty reference of the epithets major and minor
alone. Single, precise, and discriminative words would on every
account be far better than these combinations. The term *propositio*
was the designation of the major premise of a syllogism, from the
days of Cicero downwards, with few exceptions. Among these exceptions are Quintilian who uses *intentio*, Boëthius who sometimes uses
sumptum, and Rodolphus Agricola who employs *expositio*. *Assump-
tio* was even more generally the designation of the second proposition
of the syllogism—the minor premise. So that, in fact, when the two
first members of a syllogism are not (after Aristotle) called the major

2. That the sumption be universal.

In the *second figure*, the middle term is the predicate in each premise ; *e.g.*,—

> No liar is to be believed.
>
> Every good man is to be believed.
>
> Therefore—No good man is a liar.

and minor proposition, the terms *proposition* and *assumption* are generally found employed to express them. These terms all more or less shadow forth the relation of subordination which exists between these parts of the syllogism. This relation is, however, far more aptly and explicitly denoted by the correlative terms *sumption* and *subsumption ;* and as we have already assume and assumption with other cognate terms, there is no reason why we should not also avail ourselves of the convenient terms subsumption and subsume.

Even the terms sumption and subsumption are not, however, equal to the whole extent of the necessity, for between the two first members of syllogisms, in the second and third figures, there is no such relation of subordination as they express, so that it is only by courtesy to custom that these terms can be applied to them. The same is true of the reasoning from wholes to wholes ; so that we still need terms of generic latitude sufficient to express the two first members of *any* syllogism. For all ordinary purposes, however, the above are sufficient. They have the great merit of being single and precise epithets ; and after what has been said, their use in the figures cannot be misunderstood.

The only thorough-going and consistent attempt ever made, that I am aware of, to render the technicalities of logical science into English terms, was that of Ralph Lever, Dean of Durham. In his logical treatise, entitled, " The Art of Reason, rightly termed *Witcraft*, teaching a perfect way to argue and dispute," and published in London in the year 1573, he expressly undertakes to accomplish this. He explains and defends his procedure in the preface, (*forespeach*,) of which the following extract may be taken as a specimen :—" For trial hereof I wish you to aske any English man, who understandeth neither Greek nor Latin, what he conceiveth in his mind when he heareth this word, a *backset*, and what he doth conceive when he heareth this term, a *predicate*. And doubtlesse he must confesse, if

The laws of this figure are—

1. That one of the two premises be negative ; and consequently that the conclusion be so.

2. That the sumption be universal.

In the *third figure,* the middle term is the subject in both premises ; *e.g.,*—

> All man is risible.
> All man is capable of science.
> Therefore—Some capable of science is risible.

The laws of this figure are—

1. That the subsumption be affirmative.

2. That the conclusion be particular.

In the *fourth figure,* the middle term is the predicate in the sumption and the subject in the subsumption ; *e.g.,*—

> All oranges are fruit.
> All fruit is refreshing
> Therefore—Some refreshing things are oranges.

he consider the matter aright, or have any sharpnesse of wit at al, that by a *backset* he conceiveth a thing that must be set after, and by a *predicate* that he doth understand nothing at all." He accordingly renders every (or certainly almost every) technical term of common use in logic by combinations of purely Saxon words. We will give both as a specimen of his coinage, and as pertinent to the purpose of the present note, the terms which he has used to express the different members of the syllogism. These are *foresay* and *endsay, first foresay,* (major premise,) *second foresay,* (minor premise,) *endsay,* (conclusion ;) or, in his own words,—" The two first shewsayes (propositions) that are placed in a reason by rule, are called foresayes—the third may be termed an endsay." (*Art of Witcraft,* p. 103.) These terms are sufficiently general for *any* form of syllogism ; but as the technical terms of the science are all of Latin derivation, Saxon compounds cannot be accepted.]

The laws of this figure are—

1. When the sumption is affirmative, the subsumption is always universal.

2. When the subsumption is affirmative, the conclusion is particular.

3. If either of the premises be negative, the sumption must be universal.*

MOOD.—What is called mood is a modification of a syllogism, determined by the quantity and quality of the propositions of which it is composed. All the figures admit of syllogistic variations thus determined. Four kinds of propositions are, according to logicians, afforded by the various possible combinations of quantity and quality. Universal affirmative, (A)—universal negative, (E)—particular affirmative, (I)—particular negative, (O.) And as there are three propositions in every syllogism, all the possible combinations of quality and quantity will be sixty-four. Of these sixteen are excluded from having negative premises; twelve from having particular premises; twelve more for having a negative premise with an affirmative conclusion; eight, from one of the premises being particular, but the conclusion universal; and, finally, four more from having a negative conclusion where both premises were affirmative. There are thus left twelve moods. Of these, however, for various particular reasons, six

* These laws are taken from the *Port-Royal Logic*, but they are substantially the same in most logical systems.

only are allowable in each figure, making twenty-four in all. Of these, however, five are again thrown out of account from having a particular conclusion where a universal is competent. There thus remain in all the figures only nineteen valid moods. These are embodied in the well-known lines—" *Barbara Celarent,*" &c.

REDUCTION.—Logicians, though altogether ignorant of the true character of figure, strictly so called, seem always, however, to have felt, that the form of reasoning in the first figure was more exact than in the three others, and the conclusion afforded by it more logically direct and satisfactory. They have, accordingly, devised a process for changing syllogisms of the three other figures into those of the first. *This process is technically termed reduction.* Reduction is twofold—

1. *Reductio ostensiva.*—This is effected by the conversion and transposition of propositions ; *e.g.*— *Disamis* of the third figure into *Darii* of the first.

Disamis.

Some tyrant is unjust.
All tyrants are cruel.
Some cruel is unjust.

Here the major premise and conclusion are first converted, and then the premises transposed ; thus—

Darii.

All tyrants are cruel.
Some unjust are tyrants.
Some unjust are cruel.

2. *Reductio ad impossibile.*—This is effected, not directly, but indirectly, by proving that the contradictory of the syllogism under examination is something impossible or absurd. This is accomplished by taking the contradictory of the conclusion with one of the premises, and inferring from these the contradictory of the other premise—in the second figure the contradictory of the minor—in the third the contradictory of the major premise. Thus— *Baroco* of the second into *Barbara* of the first figure:

Baroco.

All rational is risible.
Some animals are not risible.
Some animals are not rational.

Barbara.

All rational is risible.
All animal is rational.
All animal is risible.

Such, on the common doctrine, is a short account of syllogistic figure, mood, and reduction. We go on *to state generally some of the defects by which this doctrine is characterised.*

1. *The whole doctrine is cumbrous and unsatisfactory.*

In addition to the general laws which are laid down by logicians as governing all syllogisms, and the various kinds of syllogism which have been signalised, we have here what are represented as four new essential variations of the syllogistic form, each

guarded by its own complement of special laws—
forming altogether a code of particular rules for the
detection of petty offences, which is certainly sufficiently intricate and perplexing. Now, the necessity
of these empirical laws is not attempted to be vindicated on any thorough-going logical principle ; and
until it be, we think their minute and multiform character is valid ground of objection.   No right, moreover, has been established, that we know of, for the
three last figures themselves, to occupy the place
they do as true variations of the syllogistic form, except a prescriptive right, which in logic, where so
many false principles have for so long usurped authority, and so many true ones been ignored, when un-
accompanied by any other, is rather ground for suspicion than otherwise.   Accordingly, till a better
right than this be shown why they should be considered independent syllogistic forms, their want of
conformity to recognised law in their procedure, and
the indirectness of their conclusions, furnish good
ground of dissatisfaction with their logical position.

Next we have *the moods* in each figure—the test-
ing of the true moods in each by its particular laws
—these laws determining the exclusion in one figure
of moods that are held valid in another ; and this
exclusion thus necessarily producing a numerical difference of moods in different figures.   That what is a
true mood in one figure should be a false one in
another, is, to say the least, unsatisfactory.

And, finally, we have the doctrine of REDUCTION—
the most cumbrous and unsatisfactory part of the
whole.   The first half of the process involves a procedure opposed to other parts of the common doctrine, since it admits the transposition of premises
at will.   (Of this, however, more presently.)   The
procedure of the second half of the process is almost
ingeniously perplexed and cumbrous, and when
accomplished, so far as we see, answers no end whatever.   We form an entirely new syllogism, which
throws no light upon the old ; illustrates no part
that was before obscure ; gives us, indeed, no knowledge at all.   The old figure remains with its irregularity (if it had any) uncorrected ; with its illegal
aspect (if that were its vice) unremoved.   It is, in
short, cumbrous without the justification of being
useful ; and most unsatisfactory it should seem in
the mere wantonness of being so, since it cannot
urge the extenuating plea of necessity.

2. *This doctrine is inconsistent.*

We begin by noticing the inconsistency displayed
in the discrimination of moods on the common doctrine.   We have seen that the principle on which
the discrimination of moods proceeds, is the difference in quantity and quality of the propositions
which constitute a syllogism.   In order to determine a variation of mood in a syllogism, one at least
of its propositions must differ, in one or other of these
respects, from all other co-ordinate moods.   If in

two syllogisms of a given figure there be no difference, either of quantity or quality in the propositions of which they are composed, these syllogisms
are logically reckoned as one and the same : there
is in this case no modal variation.   This at least is
the common doctrine, if that doctrine have any
meaning.   In opposition thereto, however, we have
discriminated as true varieties *in the second figure*—

Camestres.

All wise men are truly happy.
No intemperate man is truly happy.
No intemperate man is a wise man.

Cesare.

No intemperate man is truly happy.
All wise men are truly happy.
No wise man is an intemperate man.

And in the third figure—

Datisi.

Every true patriot is brave.
Some true patriots are persecuted.
Some that are persecuted are brave.

Disamis.

Some true patriots are persecuted.
Every true patriot is brave.
Some who are brave are persecuted.

Now, the syllogisms thus given under each figure
have no difference whatever in the quantity or qua-

lity of their propositions ; they are, therefore, according to the theory of logicians, *the same*. Practically, however, they have been considered from time immemorial as distinct ; as constituting valid variations of syllogistic form under each figure. If this be so, the principle on which the discrimination of mood avowedly proceeds is, at least, implicitly given up, and another is introduced—*that of the transposition of propositions ;* for it is on this principle alone that the syllogisms given above can be vindicated as distinct. If, however, the transposed order of propositions be recognised as affording a worthy principle for the discrimination of syllogistic difference, then a number of new forms will emerge, of which logicians have taken no account. The catalogue of syllogistic variations will immediately be swelled far beyond its present limits, since every existing variety is capable, by the transposition of its propositions, of receiving a fivefold amplification. It is clear, however, that the transposed order of propositions affords no principle of any scientific value in the discrimination of syllogisms ; and, what is more to the present purpose, it is equally clear, that whatever be its value, it is one which has not been recognised by logicians, since they have not even incidentally adverted to it in the exposition of their doctrine. The principle of modal variation on that doctrine is manifestly the difference of propositions in quantity and quality. In obvious inconsistency, however, with this recognised law, there remain the syllogisms stated above.

But a more important, if not more glaring inconsistency remains to be noticed *in the correlative doctrines of figures and reduction.*[*] The opposition here is so great that it seems to us truly marvellous that they should ever have existed together. They appear mutually and triumphantly to destroy each other. We will endeavour to explain what we mean in a few words. *The inconsistency may be stated thus :* In the cogency of formal proof there can be no degrees. Logic, it need hardly be repeated, is a formal science, proceeding from, and determined through its whole course by, *the laws of thought.* This being the case, every true variation of the syllogistic form will afford a conclusion equally valid and direct ; since a form of reasoning is true only as determined by a law of thought, and the laws of thought are equally universal and imperative. If a given syllogistic form be determined as original and essential, it is already self-sufficient ; it needs no help, it can receive none. No process can be devised for bestowing on its conclusion a higher validity than that which it possesses of its own inherent right. For, as we have said of formal proof, there can be no degrees of cogency. In every case it is alike valid and direct. With

---

* Throughout the ensuing discussion we use "*figure*" simply in the sense of *figure strictly so called, i.e.,* to the exclusion of the first, in order to avoid constant circumlocution.

respect, therefore, to every true variation of syllogistic form, *what is called reduction is useless.*

On the other hand, if the conclusion afforded by a syllogism be one-sided and indirect, and its form, therefore, apparently imperfect or irregular, there is good ground for suspicion that there is some complexity or confusion in its form, which it is necessary to disentangle or clear away before the syllogism emerges in its purity, and before, therefore, its true form can be correctly determined. When this confusion or complexity is removed—and it is the office of logical analysis to accomplish this—the syllogism will appear in its real character, and naturally fall under some determinate class of recognised syllogistic form. To such a syllogism what is called *reduction* is obviously inapplicable, since we cannot talk of reducing a syllogism of a given form to itself. Thus, on either alternative, the doctrine of *reduction* seems alike inapplicable, if not impossible. *If the syllogistic form be essential, reduction is useless; if it be accidental, it is absurd.*

Logicians, however, so far as we can understand the common doctrine, seem to have chosen the former, and perhaps milder alternative,—that the figures are true variations of syllogistic form. If this were not the case, it would have been explicitly stated ; and, in fact, the doctrine of reduction itself is at once the evidence that they so regarded them, and the proof that this is not their true character. If they did not so consider them,

it is difficult to account for the existence of reduction
at all ; for it is introduced expressly to strengthen
the position of the figures, and to vindicate to their
conclusions the highest validity.   Not clearly com-
prehending the true nature of the figures, their doctrine respecting them was imperfect.   They determined that they were true syllogistic varieties, but
still felt that this was not perfectly satisfactory—that
there was something wanting in their doctrine ; and
in order to bestow upon it the requisite completeness,
they unhappily fell upon the doctrine of reduction—
a process which, so far from establishing the truth of
that which it was introduced to demonstrate, is the
clearest evidence of its falsehood.   In fact, we cannot but regard the whole doctrine as the work of a
most perverse and suicidal ingenuity.   Introduced as
a bulwark of strength to the figures, it becomes the
very mockery of their weakness, and affords its sus-
taining aid only in the moment of their dissolution.
For we certainly cannot understand how a doubtful
variation of syllogistic form is vindicated as valid and
essential through a process which accomplishes its
destruction ; in other words, by being changed into
a form, of the validity of which there is no question.

But even granting that the whole doctrine was,
in the main, correct, it is chargeable with inconsistencies of detail ; such as the explicit recognition at
one time of a determinate major and minor premiss
in the figures, and the implicit denial of this at an-

other. These, however, it is not necessary now to notice. Suffice it to have shown that the related doctrines of figure and reduction are most seriously inconsistent, if not mutually destructive of each other.

3. *The common doctrine is destructive of the science itself.*

We bring this charge against the common doctrine —and it is the gravest of all—that it is destructive of the science, by implicitly, at least, impeaching the veracity of the laws of thought upon which the science is founded.

This may be illustrated in one or two ways. In all categorical syllogisms the reasoning is founded upon the law of identity, that a whole is identical with all its parts, a concept with its attributes, &c., and thus that " a part of a part is a part of the whole." The reasoning, therefore, if it be valid, always of necessity involves the subordination of one part to a whole through a larger part.*

* [This statement requires some modification ; for, on the law of identity, the reasoning from wholes to wholes is as competent as that from parts to wholes. By this law we are entitled to infer the relation of identity between two wholes, from the perception that they stand in this relation to a common third whole, just as certainly as we are to infer the relation of inclusion between a given whole and part, from the perception that these stand in the same relation to a common third part ; *e.g.*, the reasoning all B is all A, all C is all B, therefore all C is all A, is just as competent as the reasoning all B is A, all C is B, therefore all C is A. Taken absolutely, therefore, the objection stated in the text will not stand the test of criticism. Considered relatively to the common doctrine, it is, however, valid. On that doctrine all direct formal reasoning from wholes to wholes

Now, the common doctrine recognises the figures strictly so called as ultimate varieties of syllogistic form ; implicitly, at least, declares that they are simple forms, and their reasoning valid as it stands. But in these figures there is no subordination of lesser parts to wholes through larger parts.

It is therefore clear that if the law, according to which all true reasoning is affirmed to proceed, enjoins this subordination, but that there are found, and recognised as valid, forms in which there is no such subordination—that the law is no longer trustworthy ; for having proved mendacious once, its character of necessity and universality has departed, and it may deceive again.   Thus, implicitly at least, the main foundation of all reasoning is cut away.

Again, we have seen in the common doctrine the numerical inequality of the moods under different figures.   In each figure some mood is determined as valid which is ignored by the rest.   Thus throughout the whole scheme moods are retained as true at one time which are rejected as false at another.

Now, what is the test by which the validity and

is impossible.   For a direct reasoning from wholes to wholes is only possible through the express quantification of the predicate, which the forms and rules of the common doctrine alike forbid.   In every reasoning which obeys these rules, the extent of some one term in the syllogism is necessarily left indeterminate, so that its identity of extent with any other term cannot be formally inferred.   On the common doctrine, the reasoning is thus necessarily from parts to wholes.   Taken with this explanation, therefore, the statement in the text may stand.]

invalidity of any and every variety of syllogism is determined ? No other *than its obedience to, or violation of, the laws of thought.* If a syllogism agrees with these laws, it is true ; if not, it is false. This criterion imperatively determines every possible variation of syllogistic form. If a syllogism be true to the laws of thought in its formal essence, no accidental irregularity or transposition in the arrangement of its parts can render it invalid ; if it be not thus true in the inward essence of form, no outward regularity of expression can supply the wanting validity. In other words, what the laws of thought allow, no schematic difference can ever ignore ; what the laws of thought condemn, no schematic variation can ever successfully vindicate.

In direct opposition to all this stands the common doctrine. Judged by the above standard, its whole procedure is most illegal. In its admissions and exclusions of syllogistic variety it is equally capricious and empirical ; and throughout it is consistently regardless of the great laws by which the whole process, as a logical procedure, must be ever determined. We find a certain mood rejected under a given figure—we presume because it is invalid ; but it can be invalid only because it violates the laws of thought. Presently after we find this same mood reappearing in another figure, and recognised as scientifically true. What the laws of thought erewhile condemned, the schematic difference now tri-

umphantly interposes to allow.   What we had supposed to be rejected from the science as logically false,
now boldly returns under express scientific sanction.

Thus, on the common doctrine, *the accidents of
arrangement* triumph over the *essentials of form :*
the *contingencies of expression* are of higher authority
than the *necessities of thought.*   In a formal science
we have its accidental arrangement actually dethroning its essential principles ; contingent and
particular irregularities boldly usurping that authority, through the legitimate exercise of which they
would have been themselves exiled,—that authority
through the recognition of which alone the science
can be preserved—the authority of *law necessary
and universal.*

If the procedure which issues in these results be
competent, then it is evident that logic exists no
longer ; for the destruction of the science is obviously involved in the destruction of the laws on
which it is exclusively founded.   And this destruction of the laws of thought is, as we have shown, in
effect accomplished by the common doctrine, in the
practical contradictions of these which its procedure
involves.   It thus implicitly contains in it principles
which, if fully developed, would overthrow logical
science.

We have thus seen amongst the more general defects which belong to the common doctrine, that it
is practically cumbrous and unsatisfactory ; that it

is theoretically inconsistent ; and that it involves principles destructive to the science itself. The special falsity and uselessness of this doctrine will appear more fully in detail under the division to which we now proceed.

ii. *To state the one supreme canon of the new analytic, which potentially contains the whole doctrine of categorical syllogisms, and then to develop from it some parts of that doctrine.*

That canon is—" What worse relation of subject and predicate subsists between either of two terms and a common third term, with which both are related, and one at least positively so—that relation subsists between these two terms themselves."

This canon, as we have said, involves the whole doctrine of categorical syllogisms ; determines every kind of such syllogisms ; and is to them an all-sufficient and exhaustive code of law, observing which none can be formally invalid.

We have now to show, in conformity with the purpose of this essay in general, and its third division in particular, the influence which the principle of a quantified predicate has in accomplishing the reduction of syllogistic rules to this single canon.

And here it is obvious at once, that before any such reduction of the general laws of these syllogisms can take place, the special laws which govern particular classes of such syllogisms must be dealt with.   In fact, the condition of the possibility of any such reduction of the general laws is the annihilation of the special laws.   Whatever, therefore, tends to effect the abolition of these special laws, (laws of the several figures, to wit,) tends directly to facilitate that simplification of syllogistic law which emerges in the single canon.   The principle of a quantified predicate directly contributes to accomplish this, by proving the falsity and uselessness of these special rules.

For example, the laws of the *first figure* are—*that the sumption be universal, and*—*that the subsumption be affirmative.*   Quantify the predicate, however, and neither of these laws hold.

First rule falsified.

Some men are some fleet-footed.

All rational is all man.

Some rational is some fleet-footed.

Second rule falsified.

All idealists are some philosophers.

No sensualist is any idealist.

No sensualist is some philosopher.

The laws of *the second figure* are—*that one of the premises be negative, and*—*that the sumption be universal.*   To these the principle of a quantified predicate immediately applies, and falsifies them—

First rule falsified.

All risible is all man.

All philosophers are some men.

All philosophers are some risible.

Second rule falsified.

Some mortal is all man.
All rational is all man.
All rational is some mortal.

These examples may serve to illustrate specially
the influence which the principle of a quantified predicate has upon these laws.   It is to be remarked,
however, generally, that these laws exist only in consequence of a defective logical analysis, and apply
only to such an imperfection.   When the analysis,
therefore, is complete, these laws naturally fall away
as henceforth useless and inapplicable.   The recognition of a quantified predicate and of the true nature
of figure renders this analysis complete.   Thus the
principle of a quantified predicate co-operating with
the true doctrine of figure, sweeps away for ever from
logic, as an encumbrance, all these special laws.   The
special laws being swept aside, the way is prepared
for the reduction of the general.   And this reduction effected, there emerges the supreme canon as
given above.   This canon, it is obvious, may be
again easily evolved into those general laws of which
it is the compend.   We may take as an example the
two most general laws of categorical syllogisms.

1. *That both premises be not negative.*   This is expressed in the canon by the clause—" With which
both are related, *and one at least positively so.*"

2. *That the middle term be distributed in one at
least of the premises; and it is of no consequence*

whether it be distributed as the subject or the predicate.

The first part of this law is expressed in the canon by the clause—" *related to a common middle term.*" If it be common to both it must be distributed.   The latter part of the law is expressed in the clause— " What worse relation of subject and predicate subsists between *either of two terms and a common third term.*". The common third term may thus be related to the two other terms either as subject or predicate.

It would be by no means difficult to evolve in the same manner the canon into the six more general syllogistic laws commonly given by logicians.   The relation of these laws to the different clauses of the supreme canon is, however, manifest, and therefore need not be formally evolved here.

We pass on, then, to consider this canon in another aspect.   We said that it determined every kind of categorical syllogism.

We shall endeavour to illustrate this;—

1. *Syllogisms differ with respect to the wholes in which they proceed.*

We have already said that all reasoning (deductive, that is, to which, when not otherwise specified, we always refer when speaking of reasoning in general) is from whole to part ; but as there are two kinds of logical wholes and parts, there will naturally be two kinds of reasoning, corresponding severally to these different quantities.   These wholes are—the *meta-*

physical or comprehensive whole ; and the *logical or extensive* whole. A syllogism proceeding in the former is a comprehensive syllogism, in the conclusion of which the subject is the greatest whole, and the predicate the smallest part. A syllogism proceeding in the latter whole is an extensive syllogism, in the conclusion of which the subject is the smallest part, and the predicate the greatest whole. These different kinds of syllogism, distinguished by the different kinds of wholes in which they proceed, are determined by the first clause of the canon—" *What worse relation of subject and predicate subsists between two terms,*" &c. In the whole of comprehension the predicate is worse than the subject, since it is a part in relation to a whole; in the counter whole of extension, the subject is worse than the predicate, since in this quantity the predicate has become the greatest whole, and the subject the smallest part.

2. *Syllogisms differ with respect to figure.*

The variation of figure arises, as we have seen, from the various positions of the middle term in relation to the extremes. This variation is evidently determined in the canon by the clause—" *What relation subsists between either of two terms and a common third term.*"

But here it is necessary to go somewhat more fully into detail. We shall therefore return to the canon presently.

In considering figure somewhat more closely, we shall notice ;—

a. The true nature of the figures.

We have seen that the figures, strictly so called, are regarded by logicians as true and original variations of the syllogistic form. We have seen also some of the inconsistencies which such a doctrine involves: enough certainly to beget a suspicion that it could not be the true one. We were thus led to suppose that there must be some confusion or complexity in the figures which it is necessary to remove before the true form of their reasonings could be seen in its ultimate purity and exactness. What this confusion or complexity is, we now proceed explicitly to show, by stating and illustrating the true nature of the figures.*

" The figures (strictly so called) are hybrid or mixed reasonings, in which the steps of the process are only partially expressed ; the unexpressed steps are, in general, only conversive inferences which we are entitled to make from those that are expressed."

This being the nature of figure, it follows that, since all the real steps of the process are not expressed in the reasonings, the conclusion does not of necessity follow from the expressed premises ; but the mind at once inferring and interpolating the wanting steps of the process, the conclusion follows in virtue of such inference and interpolation. When this mental interpolation is recognised, and the real premise which it constitutes is expressed, the syllogism emerges in

* Touching the value and history of this exposition, see the Appendix.

its simple form, and is at once recognised to be (through all the variations of mood and figure, strictly so called) a syllogism of the first figure. All such varieties are therefore thus shown to be, in their complex state, only unessential variations of that figure. We shall illustrate this in concrete examples through the moods of the second and third figures.

The moods of the second figure are—*Cesare, Camestres, Festino, Baroco.*

A syllogism in Cesare is—

> No unreflective man is a philosopher.
> All idealists are philosophers.
> No idealist is unreflective.

By conversive inference we obtain as the real sumption, " no philosopher is unreflective," and this interposed in the place of the ostensible sumption, produces a syllogism in *Celarent* of the first figure, *e.g.*,—

> No philosopher is unreflective.
> All idealists are philosophers.
> No idealist is unreflective.

A syllogism in Camestres is—

> All animals are sentient.
> Nothing unorganised is sentient.
> Nothing unorganised is animal.

We have already said, when speaking generally of figure, that the premises are in this syllogism transposed; and that but for such transposition it is exactly the same as *Cesare;* reversing the premises then, and dealing with it in the same manner as the last, it appears in the same form as *Celarent* of the first figure.

> Nothing sentient is unorganised.
> All animals are sentient.
> No animal is unorganised.

A syllogism in Festino is—

> No truly wise men go to extremes.
> Some truly religious men go to extremes.
> Some truly religious men are not truly wise men.

Here with the sumption converted the syllogism appears as *Ferio* of the first.

> None who go to extremes are truly wise.
> Some truly religious men go to extremes.
> Some truly religious men are not truly wise.

A syllogism in Baroco* is—

> All lilies are fragrant.
> Some flowers are not fragrant.
> Some flowers are not lilies.

Here the subsumption is to be dealt with ; and by conversive influence we obtain " *some things not fragrant are flowers.*" Interpolating this, we have a syllogism in *Darii* of the first.

---

* [The reduction of this mood was one of the standard difficulties of the logicians. It could only at best be done with difficulty, and through the clumsy process designated *ad impossibile;* nor does it accommodate itself well to this expository process of Kant's ; since after all it appears as a syllogism of the *fourth* figure rather than of the *first.*]

> All lilies are fragrant.
> Some things not fragrant are flowers.
> Some things not lilies are flowers.

The *third* figure.

We have seen, in removing the complexity of syllogisms in the second figure, that it is the sumption for the most part (that is in three out of four moods) which is affected by conversive inference ; and that that inference is made chiefly from " the absolute negation of the first notion as predicate of the second, to the absolute negation of the second notion as predicate of the first." In the third figure, on the other hand, it is the subsumption which is chiefly affected by conversive inference, and that inference is generally made " from the total or partial affirmation of a lesser notion of a greater, to the partial affirmation of the greater notion of the lesser."

The moods of the third figure are—*Darapti, Felapton, Disamis, Datisi, Bocardo, Ferison.*

A syllogism in Darapti is—

> Every good man is happy.
> Every good man fights with himself.
> Some who fight with themselves are happy.

By conversive inference we here obtain as subsumption—" *some who fight with themselves are good men ;*" and the syllogism is then in *Darii* of the first figure.

> Every good man is happy.
> Some who fight with themselves are good men.
> Some who fight with themselves are happy.

A syllogism in the second mood Felapton is—

> No man is winged.
> All men are bipeds.
> Some bipeds are not winged.

By converting the subsumption it becomes *Ferio* of the first.

> No man is winged.
> Some bipeds are men.
> Some bipeds are not winged.

A syllogism in the third mood Disamis is—

> Some patriots are persecuted.
> Every patriot is brave.
> Some that are brave are persecuted.

Here the premises are first to be transposed, then converting the subsumption the syllogism appears as *Darii* of the first—

> Every patriot is brave.
> Some that are persecuted are patriots.
> Some that are persecuted are brave.

With respect to the fourth mood in the figure, *Datisi*, we have already shown that it differs from the third only in the transposition of its premises. Converting the subsumption, therefore, it appears in the same form as *Darii* of the first. We give the syllogisms together—

> All true philosophers are truly noble.
> Some true philosophers are despised.
> Some that are truly noble are despised.

All true philosophers are truly noble.
Some that are despised are true philosophers.
Some that are despised are truly noble.

A syllogism in the fifth mood Bocardo is—

Some poets are not philosophers.
All poets have genius.
Some who have genius are not philosophers.

The premises are here transposed, and the sumption converted—it then appears as *Darii*—

All poets have genius.
Some not philosophers are poets.
Some not philosophers have genius.

A syllogism in the last mood Ferison is—

No hope is unattended with pleasure.
Some hopes are delusive.
Some delusive things are attended with pleasure.

Converting the sumption it becomes *Ferio* of the first—

No hope is without pleasure.
Some delusive things are hopes.
Some delusive things are attended with pleasure.

The syllogisms of the figures, strictly so called, are thus shown to be complex reasonings, which, when cleared of their complexity, and simply expressed, *i.e.*, expressed in that form which all true reasonings must ultimately assume, in which the least part or whole is subordinated to the greatest part or whole, through a lesser part or whole—appear in their true character as syllogisms of the first figure.

We have here taken no notice of the fourth figure, not because the same process of simplification is not equally applicable to its reasonings, as to those of the second and third figures ; but because, as we shall presently explain, we do not consider it properly a figure at all.

b. The true number of the figures.

We have seen that in the common doctrine four figures are recognised as valid.* The fourth figure

---

* [The validity of the *fourth* figure as a separate form of reasoning has been often contested, but that of the other three has remained for the most part unassailed. The *third*, however, has not wholly escaped assault. It was rejected by Laurentius Valla on the ground that such a form of reasoning was never used, that there are no examples of it to be found, and as it would seem, as much as for any other reason, because it offended his eye or ear. He does not, indeed, so much reason seriously against its validity, but rather denounces it at once, and that, too, in the most lively and rhetorical manner, as in the last degree preposterous and absurd. The whole style of the rejection is quite in harmony with his wayward originality and independence, as well as with his habit of rash yet fastidious criticism. It is, indeed, but another instance of the fastidious taste of Valla, in whose eyes a sin against purity of style was a moral offence of the gravest kind, who did not scruple to correct the Latinity of Cicero, and of whose criticism it is said the Devil himself stood in such awe, that he was afraid to speak in his presence, being nervous as to the classic purity of his Latin style.

The objections of Valla to the third figure were rebutted by Lazarus Schonerus, (as quoted by Fraunce,) who adduced examples of its use from Cicero and Virgil. Its validity and usefulness were also defended against Valla by Melanchthon, who, referring to it, says, " Laurentius Valla non leviter stomachatur hoc loco, et Aristotelem tanquam capitali judicio accusat, qui hanc figuram tradiderit. Sed Valla dum nullum rixandi finem facit, sæpe etiam incurrit, ut sit ab iracundis, in illos qui nihil peccaverunt. Mihi non tam plumbeo ingenio Aris-

was, however, introduced into the science later ; and when introduced obtained a footing less secure than the other three. Some logicians, indeed, have omitted it altogether ; while others have expressly redargued its claim to be admitted as a true schematic difference. The reasons of those who opposed its admission have not, however, proved sufficiently strong to eject it finally from the science, since it reappears in the latest systems, and is recognised as logically competent. It is, nevertheless, to be rejected from logic, as being utterly deformed and useless. *Deformed*, since its premises proceed in the whole of comprehension, and its conclusion in the counter whole of extension. *Useless*, since the reasoning in both these wholes is scientifically complete without it. The fourth figure being thus rejected, the three first alone remain. These, therefore, are to be considered as exclusively competent in logic.

c. *The true canons of the figures.*

We have said that the syllogistic difference of

totcles fuisse videtur, ut nulla de causa tertiam figuram tradiderit. Est enim reperire exempla ejus figuræ, in quibus si mutes dispositionem medii, feceris totum syllogismum obscuriorem." (*Dialectica.* Paris, 1532, fol. 42.)

This extract is taken from Melanchthon's *second* logical work. His opinion in relation to this matter does not appear to have been always equally decided, since Melchior Adam says, (in his short life of him,) referring to it ; " Edidit Philippus eodem anno (1520) primum sua Dialectica in quibus *tertiam figuram syllogismorum* neque recipit, neque rejicit ; quam deinde iterata editione, an. 1528, admisit." (*Vitæ Germanorum Philosophorum.* Francof, 1706, p. 88).]

figure is determined in the supreme canon of syllogism by the clause, " What worse relation of subject and predicate subsists between either of two terms and a common third term," &c. It is obvious, that this clause determines figure ; for the syllogistic difference of figure is discriminated by the position of the middle term in relation to the extremes ; or in other words, by the " relation of subject and predicate subsisting between the two terms and a common third term."

But this clause not only determines the difference of figure, it also immediately determines all the possible varieties of such difference. For the relation of subject and predicate, subsisting between two terms and a common third term, must be either that in which the common third term is the subject of one and the predicate of the other, or that in which it is the predicate of both, or that in which it is the subject of both. No other is possible. Now, these three possible variations of relation determine at once the number of the figures and the canons by which they are regulated. For the number of different figures can only answer to the number of different relations ; and the evolution of these different relations in detail will be the expression of the laws by which the figures thus discriminated are severally governed.

These relations are—

I. *That in which the common third term is the*

subject of one of the terms, and the predicate of the other.

This constitutes the first figure alike in extension and comprehension.

First in Extension.

B is A	Here B, the third term, is the subject of
C is B	(that is to say, contained *under*) A,
C is A	the one term; and the predicate of
	(that is to say, contains *under* it) C,
	the other term.

So in Comprehension.

C is B	Here B, the middle term, is the predi-
B is A	cate of (that is to say, comprehended
C is A	*in*) C, the one term; and the subject
	of (that is to say, comprehends *in* it)
	A, the other term.

The canon of this figure is—" In so far as two notions or terms are related, either both positively, or one positively and the other negatively, to a common third term, of which the one is subject and the other predicate,—these two notions are related positively or negatively to each other as subject and predicate."

II. *That in which the common third term is the predicate of both the other terms.*

This constitutes the second figure, and that (contrary to the logicians) is either of affirmative or of negative syllogisms.

Affirmative.	*Negative.*
All A is all B.	All A is all B.
All C is some B.	No C is any B.
All C is some A.	No C is any A.

The canon of this figure is—" In so far as two terms or notions, both subjects, are either both positively, or the one positively and the other negatively, related to a common predicate,—in so far are they either positively or negatively subject and predicate, and that indifferently of each other."

III. *That in which the third term is the subject of both the other terms.*

This constitutes the third figure, and that (also contrary to the logicians) in syllogisms with either universal or particular conclusions.

Universal.	*Particular.*
All B is some A.	All B is all A.
All B is all C.	Some B is some C.
All C is some A.	Some C is some A.

The canon of this figure is—" In so far as two notions or terms, both predicates, are either each positively, or the one positively and the other negatively, related to a common subject,—in so far are they positively or negatively subject and predicate, and this indifferently of each other."

The relation of the middle term in the second and third figures explains how it is that these figures have no determinate major or minor premise, and two indifferent conclusions. There can be no determinate major or minor premise ; *for a determinate major premise* is one in which the middle term is compared with the greatest notion, and determined by it ; *a determinate minor premise,* one in which the middle term is compared with the smallest notion, and determines it. The middle notion thus always is in the former *determined,* in the latter *determining.* Now, in the second and third figures there can be no such relation of determination. In one the middle term determines both the premises, in the other it is determined by both. Hence, since there is no determinate major or minor premise, it is manifest that we may have two indifferent conclusions ; for we may, in the second figure, indifferently predicate one subject of the other, and in third the one predicate of the other.

In the first figure, again, it is equally clear that there is such a relation of determination. In it the reasoning is perfect, proceeding from the largest whole through a lesser whole to the least whole. The first figure accordingly has a determinate major and minor premise, and one immediate conclusion.

d. The true relations of the figures.

We have already spoken of the two wholes in which reasoning proceeds—the whole of comprehension and that of extension—the characteristic of the former being that the predicate is contained *in the subject,* of the latter that the subject is contained *under the predicate.* This being remembered, it will appear that in the second figure, where the middle term as predicate contains both the subjects *under it, extension* will predominate.   In the third, where the middle term as subject is contained under, and therefore *comprehends in* it both the predicates, *comprehension* will prevail. In the first figure, again, where the middle term is both subject and predicate, extension and comprehension balance each other.   The first figure is indifferently competent to either.

Reasoning, however, proceeds not only in different wholes, but in different *aspects* of the same whole. We may, it is evident, regard any whole, considered as the complement of its parts, in either of two ways ; for we may, on the one hand, look from the whole to the parts, and reason accordingly downwards ; or, on the other hand, look from the parts to the whole they constitute, and reason accordingly upwards. The former of these reasonings is called *deductive*, the latter *inductive*.   *Deductive* reasoning is founded on the maxim—" What belongs to the containing whole belongs also to the contained parts :" *Induction* on the contrary maxim—" What belongs to the constituent parts belongs also to the constituted whole." Thus in deductive reasoning the whole is stated first, and what is affirmed of it is affirmed of the parts it contains ; in other words, a general law is laid down, and predicated of the particular instances to which it applies.   In inductive reasoning the parts are first stated, and what is predicated of them is also predicated of the whole they constitute ; in other words, the particular instances are first stated as facts, and then the law they constitute is evolved.

This being the nature of these counter and correlative reasonings, it appears to us, that though each kind is competent in either whole, (extension or comprehension,) yet that the reasoning in the whole of extension is more naturally allied to the *deductive*, and that in comprehension to the *inductive*.   For, in the whole of extension, the reasoning proceeds from the general to the special—from the abstract to the concrete—from general laws to the particular instances which are contained under them ; while in that of comprehension, on the other hand, the reasoning proceeds from the special to the general— from the concrete to the abstract—from the particular instances to the general laws, whose operation they exemplify.

The special adaptation of comprehension for inductive, and of extension for deductive reasoning, might be illustrated more fully in detail, and on other grounds ; but it may perhaps suffice to have indicated the relation between the two kinds of reasoning, and the two counter wholes in which they proceed.

Considering these kinds of reasoning in relation to the figures, it will appear, then, that since extension prevails in the second, that will be so far more suitable for deductive reasoning ; and since comprehension prevails in the third, that figure will so far be more

adapted for inductive reasoning ; while, since extension and comprehension prevail equally in the first,
that figure will be equally fitted for either kind of
reasoning.*

* [The relation of the figures to these different kinds of reasoning
will be best illustrated by an example. We will take first the second
figure :—

Deductive reasoning : Quantity of extension.

Fig. II. $\begin{cases} \text{Endowed with reason is all man.} \\ \text{European, Asiatic, African, American, are all man.} \\ \text{European, Asiatic, African, American, are endowed with} \\ \quad \text{reason.} \end{cases}$

Here the reasoning is *deductive*, for the law is first enounced, the
individual instances are next brought under it, and it is then affirmed
of them ; it is *extensive*, for it proceeds from the wider notion through
the narrower to the individual.   Let us now take the same terms and
treat them inductively, beginning with the individuals.   The reasoning will then be in the whole of comprehension, and will naturally
appear in the form of the third figure :—

Inductive reasoning : Quantity of comprehension.

Fig. III. $\begin{cases} \text{European, Asiatic, African, American, are all man.} \\ \text{European, Asiatic, African, American, are endowed with} \\ \quad \text{reason.} \\ \text{Endowed with reason is all man.} \end{cases}$

Here the reasoning is *inductive*, for beginning with the individuals
in the premises, we arrive at the law (with which we started in the
previous syllogism) in the conclusion ; it is *comprehensive* or *intensive*, for it proceeds from the concrete to the abstract, from a greater
totality of attribute to a less.   In other words, in either quantity
(extensive or intensive) we reason from the greatest whole ; but in
the quantity of extension the greatest whole is the most abstract
notion, (*i.e.*, the widest law,) whereas in that of comprehension, the
greatest whole is the most concrete notion, (*i.e.*, the individual instance.)   But proceeding thus from the widest law the reasoning
is necessary deductive, while on the other hand, proceeding from
the individual instance, it is as necessarily inductive.

The second and third figures are indeed naturally respectively connected with deductive and inductive

We may give the same example in the first figure, to illustrate (what will now be quite obvious) that it is indifferently competent to either reasoning :—

Fig. I.

Deductive reasoning : Quantity of extension.

All man is endowed with reason.
European, Asiatic, African, American, are all man.
European, Asiatic, African, American, are endowed with reason.

Inductive reasoning : Quantity of comprehension.

European, Asiatic, African, American, are all man.
All man is endowed with reason.
European, Asiatic, African, American, are endowed with reason.

I need scarcely say, that at the time of writing the essay, I was quite unaware that any of these special relations of the figures had been noticed by logicians.   I find, however, that Wilson, in his " *Rule of Reason*," (1580,) has, among other remarks tracing the use of the figures, the following :—" *Use of the third figure :* This figure profiteth much in provoking particular things, and gathering of conjectures in causes that are doubtful, when probability only, and no assured knowledge, boulteth out the truth of a matter.   And because several things (individuals) come sonest to our senses, we use suche gathering moste commonly, and by triall of particular causes, assure ourselves of the truthe generally."   Again, " when we make an argument and procede from the general word (genus) to the kind (species), it is in the first figure, and even by our reason we learn this, that if the greater bee not, the lesse cannot bee."

" When we procede from the kinde to the general, making the conclusion particular, the argument is in the third figure.   And this is for ever true, that when the kinde is rehearsed, the generall must needes followe."   (Fol. 30-1.)   This, however, is little beyond a more explicit statement of what is commonly said of the third figure, that it is a reasoning from the special.]

reasoning ; for in the second we judge the likeness or unlikeness of two parts, as they are contained or not contained by a common whole ; while in the third we judge the likeness or unlikeness of two wholes, as they severally contain or do not contain common parts.

3. *Syllogisms differ with respect to mood.*

The syllogistic variety of mood arises from the different quality and quantity of propositions, and this difference is determined by the supreme canon in the clause—" *What worse relation of subject and predicate,*" &c., since a negative quality is a worse relation than a positive, and a particular quantity a worse relation than a universal.

Logicians, however, in their enumeration of moods, as we have seen, have taken into account only one quantity of propositions ; have considered the subject as quantified to the exclusion of the predicate ; and have, in so doing, deformed their science by excluding from it many valid forms of reasoning—forms which logic, if it be an exact science, and its analysis of the form of thought exhaustive, is bound to recognise and vindicate as valid.

It is the design of the " new analytic " that its analysis shall be thus exhaustive ; and it vindicates its title by discovering and developing, in its various relations, an element of formal thought which had remained undeveloped, if not unrecognised, in every previous analysis. That element is, as we have said, the express quantification of the predicate, the true application of which recalls to the science many true forms of reasoning, the date of whose logical proscription may be reckoned as coeval with that of the science itself.

We shall proceed briefly to vindicate these forms. Logicians, combining the quality of a proposition with the quantity of its subject, reckon in all four kinds of propositions ; and combining these propositions in every possible way, evolve sixty-four moods. But it is clear, that if the quantity of the predicate be taken into account, the various kinds of propositions discriminated by quantity and quality will be doubled in number, and a proportionate increase effected in the number of possible moods ; for we shall now have eight kinds of propositions, viz., four affirmative :—

> Definite, affirmative, definite.
> Definite, affirmative, indefinite.
> Indefinite, affirmative, definite.
> Indefinite, affirmative, indefinite.

And in the same manner, four negative propositions. With this increase in the number of propositions, we need new symbols by which to designate them. We may, however, still retain the old notation A. I. E. O., and express the new forms by combining the letters into diphthongs, or placing them within brackets, as occasion may require ; *e.g.,*—

> Definite, affirmative, indefinite = (AI.)
> Indefinite, negative, definite = Œ, &c.

This increase in the number of propositions to be combined effects of course a great increase in the number of moods resulting from such combination. Of the possible moods thus given, a number are invalidated by the clause of the canon, "*one at least positively so*," from having two negative premises. A number more are excluded by the clause, "*a common third term*," from the middle term being undistributed. Throwing these out of account, together with some others having particular conclusions where universal are competent, *there remain in all thirty-six valid moods*, (twelve affirmative and twenty-four negative,) and these thirty-six are valid in each figure.

We employ the symbolical notation,* using the comma (,) to denote "some," (indefinite quantity,) and the colon (:) to denote "all," (definite quantity).

Valid moods of the first figure.

* On this system of notation, see the Appendix.

iv. A , —— : B : —— : C $\begin{cases} 1.\ \text{A}, +— : \text{B} : —— : \text{C} \\ \underline{\hspace{3cm}} \\ 2.\ \text{A}, —— : \text{B} : +— : \text{C} \end{cases}$

v. A : —— : B , —— : C $\begin{cases} 1.\ \text{A} : +— : \text{B}, —— : \text{C} \\ \underline{\hspace{3cm}} \\ 2.\ \text{A} : —— : \text{B}, +— : \text{C} \end{cases}$

vi. A : —— , B : —— : C $\begin{cases} 1.\ \text{A} : +— , \text{B} : —— : \text{C} \\ \underline{\hspace{3cm}}, \\ 2.\ \text{A} : —— , \text{B} : +— : \text{C} \end{cases}$

vii. A , —— : B , —— , C $\begin{cases} 1.\ \text{A}, +— : \text{B}, —— , \text{C} \\ \underline{\hspace{3cm}} \\ 2.\ \text{A}, —— : \text{B}, +— , \text{C} \end{cases}$

viii. A , —— , B : —— , C $\begin{cases} 1.\ \text{A}, +— , \text{B} : —— , \text{C} \\ \underline{\hspace{3cm}} \\ 2.\ \text{A}, —— , \text{B} : +— , \text{C} \end{cases}$

ix. A : —— : B , —— , C $\begin{cases} 1.\ \text{A} : +— : \text{B}, —— , \text{C} \\ \underline{\hspace{3cm}} \\ 2.\ \text{A} : —— : \text{B}, +— , \text{C} \end{cases}$

x. A , —— , B : —— : C $\begin{cases} 1.\ \text{A}, +— , \text{B} : —— : \text{C} \\ \underline{\hspace{3cm}}, \\ 2.\ \text{A}, —— , \text{B} : +— : \text{C} \end{cases}$

xi. A , —— : B , —— : C $\begin{cases} 1.\ \text{A}, +— : \text{B}, —— : \text{C} \\ \underline{\hspace{3cm}} \\ 2.\ \text{A}, —— : \text{B}, +— : \text{C} \end{cases}$

xii. A : —— , B : —— , C $\begin{cases} 1.\ \text{A} : +— , \text{B} : —— , \text{C} \\ \underline{\hspace{3cm}} \\ 2.\ \text{A} : —— , \text{B} : +— , \text{C} \end{cases}$

We have given the above syllogisms in the first figure; but they may all be easily translated into the two others.*

* [The only one of the prescribed requisites which the essay does

To recapitulate then. We set out with the principle of a quantified predicate. We have noticed some things by the way not immediately connected therewith ; but recurring to it, we have endeavoured to vindicate that principle. We have indicated its influence on propositions in abolishing the complex doctrine of conversion ; its influence on categorical syllogisms, in reducing their laws to a higher simplicity, and amplifying their valid forms,—in short, by correcting what was false, and supplying what was wanting ; and thus, by securing to logic a higher degree of formal exactness, realising for it a higher degree of scientific perfection.

not to some extent attempt to meet, is that in which it is required " to show in concrete examples, through all the moods, the unessential variation which figure makes in a syllogism." This was omitted at the time of writing through haste ; but it is so obvious, that with a little trouble, each reader may do it for himself. As an illustration, however, the following is a concrete example of the first mood, carried through all the figures :—

Fig. I.
{ All man is some animal.
Every Celt is some man.
Every Celt is some animal.

Fig. II.
{ Some animal is all man.
Every Celt is some man.
Every Celt is some animal.

Fig. III.
{ All man is some animal.
Some man is every Celt.
Some animal is every Celt.

Fig. IV.
{ Some animal is all man.
Some man is every Celt.
Some animal is every Celt.

The "*new analytic*" accomplishes this by being
true to its office, and fully investigating the form of
thought. *The form, the whole form, and nothing but
the form of thought,* is indeed the bannered motto
which it bears on its triumphant way. True to
its purpose, it advances over the whole region of
formal thought, conquering and to conquer ; destroying the false landmarks which had been set
up by the early discoverers of that territory ; re-
pressing the incursions which were continually made
into neighbouring kingdoms ; destroying the border
ground by determining for ever the frontier line ;
dethroning the potentates who had intrenched themselves in its high places, and long there exer-
cised a usurped authority ; recalling from their
long exile the true lords of the soil ; re-establish-
ing the laws on which their rights were founded, and
enforcing strict obedience to these in every province
of the empire. Thus, though in some respects its
path is as the path of the destroyer, in a higher and
truer sense it is the path of peace ; for through its
instrumentality there breaks at length upon this long
distracted region the golden age of simplicity and
order. And anarchy, the result of laws neglected
and rights ignored, is for ever abolished in the esta-
blishment of perfect harmony—a harmony the result
of law clearly expounded and rigidly obeyed throughout the entire empire of formal thought.

In conclusion, we are well aware of the very imperfect manner in which we have signalised those parts of the new discovery on which we have touched. We cannot, however, close without expressing the true joy we feel, (though, were the feeling less strong, we might shrink from the intrusion,) that in our country, and in our time, this discovery has been made.   We rejoice to know that one has at length arisen, able to recognise and complete the plan of the mighty builder, Aristotle,—to lay the top-stone on that fabric, the foundations of which were laid more than two thousand years ago by the master hand of the Stagirite, which, after the labours of many generations of workmen, who have from time to time built up one part here and taken down another there—remains substantially as he left it ; but which, when finished, shall be seen to be an edifice of wondrous beauty, harmony, and completeness.

APPENDIX.

No. I.

The statement made in the first page of the Essay, that " the
principle of a quantified predicate had, in its full scientific significance, been totally overlooked by logicians, and that, when
noticed at all, it had, for the most part, been referred to only to
be discarded as useless, if not to be condemned as false"—was
made, it scarcely need be said, upon a very limited acquaintance
with logical works. It was, however, the conclusion to which
my inquiries, so far as they extended, led me. I had examined
several logical treatises, and found that the majority made no reference at all to a quantified predicate, that the few who noticed
it, (two of which are quoted,) treated it in the manner described
in the text; while, so far as my reading extended, I had not
found a single instance in which it was admitted in any form.
Since writing the Essay, I have naturally been curious in my
occasional logical reading to mark any references which might
be made to this subject; and as the result of a somewhat fuller
knowledge of the historical development of the science, I am able
to establish, upon somewhat wider evidence, the general truth
of the statement made in the text. The full scientific significance of the principle certainly never has been appreciated. It
has been, " for the most part, rejected;" that is to say, it
has been denounced by the vast majority of logicians as

useless and false. Some exceptions, however, to this summary rejection of the principle are to be found. A few of these
I have met with, some of which as in themselves curious, and
as lying out of the way of ordinary reading, it may be worth
while explicitly to notice. In order, therefore, to place the Essay
on a level with my present knowledge, I shall briefly establish
historically the common rejection of the principle of a quantified
predicate, and then notice some of the exceptions to this treatment of it which are to be found.

I. *The common doctrine which altogether rejects the express quan-*
tification of the predicate.

This doctrine dates substantially, as do most logical truths
and heresies, from Aristotle. He refers explicitly in two
places*—in his *Book on the Doctrine of Enunciation*, and in his
Prior Analytics—to the quantification of the predicate, and
in both rejects it in a very summary manner. In the Book
touching Enunciation he says,—" Ἐπὶ δὲ τοῦ κατηγορουμένου
καθόλου τὸ καθόλου κατηγορεῖν, οὐκ ἔστιν ἀληθές· οὐδεμία γὰρ κατάφασις
ἀληθὴς ἔσται, ἐν ᾗ τοῦ κατηγορουμένου καθόλου τὸ καθόλου κατηγορεῖται
οἷον ἔστι πᾶς ἄνθρωπος πᾶν ζῶον." (*De Enunciandi Ratione*, c. vii.
§ 4.) The parallel passage in the *Prior Analytics* is as follows:
" Αὐτὸ δὲ τὸ ἑπόμενον οὐ ληπτέον ὅλον ἕπεσθαι· λέγω δ', οἷον ἀνθρώπῳ
πᾶν ζῶον, ἢ μουσικῇ πᾶσαν ἐπιστήμην· ἀλλ' ἁπλῶς μόνον ἀκολουθεῖν,
καθάπερ καὶ προτεινόμεθα· καὶ γὰρ ἄχρηστον θάτερον, καὶ ἀδύνατον,
οἷον πάντα ἄνθρωπον εἶναι πᾶν ζῶον· ἢ δικαιοσύνην ἅπαν ἀγαθόν."
(*Anal. Pri.* i. c. 27, § 9.) The quantification of the predicate is
to be absolutely rejected; such is the judgment of Aristotle on
the point.† That this judgment was given rashly and without

---

* Other references are made to the subject by Aristotle in the *Book of the*
Categories and the *Posterior Analytics*; but the above are the most decisive
passages.

† It is right to state, that the only case which is here explicitly contemplated by Aristotle, is that in which the predicate is quantified *universally.*
His dictum, however, in relation to this is not true, since we may often

due consideration is, however, manifest, both from the fact that
Aristotle himself explicitly quantifies the predicate in other parts
of his writings, as also from the fact that his formal rejection of
such quantification is unsupported by a single argument. All
that is offered in its defence is an illustration so inept and one-
sided, that its fallacy seems almost transparent. He says, in
effect, that it is impossible to quantify the predicate, because it
is false to say, *all man is all animal;* which is surely no better
as an argument than it would be to say, that it is impossible to
divide a foot into inches, because it is false to say that *one inch
is a whole foot.* With the exception of this example, and one
or two others of the same kind, Aristotle wisely abstains from
offering any defence of his hasty judgment. His wisdom in
this respect has not, however, been imitated by his followers,
who have, in various ways, endeavoured to explain and defend
the dictum of their master.

Passing over the Greek commentators, (with whose labours
I am not sufficiently familiar to enable me to speak of them
with confidence,) we come to the first, as in some respects he
still remains the best Latin expositor of Aristotle—Boëthius.
Boëthius flourished during the latter part of the fifth and the
beginning of the sixth centuries. He translated all the books
of the Organon, and wrote elaborate commentaries on more
than one, besides furnishing other and more direct contributions
to logical science in the form of original treatises. To his ver-
sions and commentaries the schoolmen were mainly indebted
for their knowledge of Aristotle; and to these, accordingly,
may be traced several of the particular interpretations which
subsequently became current in the science, and were, indeed,
for the most part authenticated as of Aristotelic origin. To determine, therefore, the opinion of Boëthius on any particular point,

quantify the predicate universally; but as he implicitly makes this case representative of the whole doctrine, it is obviously altogether false, since we
may, and must always quantify the predicate *universally* or *particularly.*

is of some importance, as it will be often found to be that which
subsequently prevailed.

He gives the point in question fuller consideration than it
receives at the hands of Aristotle; but in his treatment of it,
nevertheless, he confines himself to the same restricted aspect,
and arrives substantially at the same one-sided conclusion.
Considering exclusively the case in which the predicate is
quantified *universally*, he proves triumphantly what seems to require really very little proof, that the genus cannot receive a
mark of universal quantity when it is predicated of its species.
Commenting on the passage already quoted from the Book
touching *Enunciation*, he says as follows :—

"Quod dicit hujusmodi est:—Omnis propositio simplex duobus
terminis constat, his sæpe additur aut *universalitatis* aut *particularitatis determinatio ;* sed ad *quam partem* hæ determinationes
addantur, exponit. Videtur enim Aristoteli, prædicato termino
determinationem non oportere conjungi. In hac enim propositione, quæ est ' homo animal est,' quæritur—subjectumne debeat
cum determinatione dici, ut sit ' omnis homo animal est ;' an
prædicatum, ut sit ' homo omne animal est ;' an utrumque, ut
sit ' omnis homo omne animal est.' *Sed neutrum eorum quæ posterius dicta sunt, fieri oportet ; namque ad prædicatum nunquam
determinatio jungitur, sed ad subjectum tantum.* Neque enim verum
est dicere ' omne animal omnis homo est ;' idcirco, quoniam
omnis prædicatio, aut *major* est *subjecto*, aut *æqualis*. Ut in eo
quod dicimus, ' omnis homo animal est,' plus est animal quam
homo. Et rursus in eo quod dicimus, ' homo risibilis est,' risibile æquatur homini. Ut autem sit mínus prædicatum atque
angustius subjecto, fieri non potest. Ergo in *his predicatis* quæ
subjecto *majora* sunt, ut in eo quod est animal, perspicue *falsa*
est propositio, si determinatio universalitatis ad prædicatum
terminum ponitur. Nam si dicamus, ' homo est animal,' animal,
quod majus est homine, per hanc determinationem ad subjectum
hominem usque contrahimus ; cum non solum ad hominem, sed

ad alia quoque, nomen animalis possit aptari. Rursus, in iis quæ *æqualia* sunt, idem evenit. Nam si dicam, ' omnis homo omne risibile est,' primum, si ad *humanitatem* ipsam referam, *superfluum est adjicere determinationem.* Quod si ad *singulos* quosquam hominum, *falsa* est propositio ; nam cum dico ' omnis homo omne risibile est,' hoc videor significare, singuli homines omne risibile sunt, quod fieri non potest. *Non igitur ad prædicatum, sed ad subjectum determinatio ponenda.* Verba autem Aristotelis, hoc modo sunt, et ad hanc sententiam ducuntur :—' In his prædicatis quæ sunt universalia, his adjicere universale aliquid, ut universale prædicatum universaliter prædicatur, non est verum ;' hoc enim est quod ait. In eo vero quod prædicatur universaliter, id est, quod habet prædicatum universale, ipsum universale prædicatum [prædicare] universaliter, non est verum. In prædicato enim universali, id est, quod universale est et prædicatur, ipsum prædicatum, quod universale est, universaliter prædicare, id est, *adjecta determinatione universalitatis, non est verum. Neque enim potest fieri, ut ulla sit affirmatio vera, in qua de universali prædicato universalis determinatio prædicetur;* eisque rei notionem exemplo aperit, dicens, ' ut omnis homo omne animal est ;' hoc autem quam sit inconveniens, supra jam diximus." (*Opera Omnia. Basil.,* pp. 348, 349.)

In the opening sentence of this (corrected) extract Boëthius states the question fairly, and looks at it from a higher point of view than that in which it had been considered by Aristotle. He begins by saying, that every simple proposition is composed of two terms, that to these a determination of *universality* or *particularity* is often added, and then proceeds to inquire to which of the terms *these* determinations should be affixed. From this introduction it might reasonably have been inferred that the question would be discussed on broader grounds than those on which it had previously been treated, and that quantification in relation to the predicate would be considered in its generic latitude, and not in one of its species alone. This expectation is, however, as we have said, not fulfilled; for immediately after having said that the terms receive marks of *universality* and *particularity*, and that the inquiry is, to which of the terms these marks should be appended, Boëthius proceeds to consider the mark of *universality* alone; and decides on this restricted consideration of the matter, that the marks of quantity are to be affixed exclusively to the subject, and never to the predicate.

The whole passage is, however, curious and valuable, not only in itself, but also in its historic relation, from its having (as already hinted) determined in effect nearly all that was subsequently said by others on the subject. There is not, I think, in all the subsequent refutations of a quantified predicate which have been attempted, a single argument which is not substantially contained in this quotation.

The next name of authority after Boëthius is that of the Arabian Averroes, who, from the extent and value of his labours, as expositor of Aristotle, was called *The Commentator*, κατ᾽ ἐξοχήν. He flourished in the twelfth century, and by his almost incredible devotion to Aristotle, and his unwearied zeal in expounding and epitomising his works, contributed not a little to promote the complete ascendency which the peripatetic philosophy subsequently obtained.

Averroes treats the point in question with much greater brevity than Boëthius, but arrives at precisely the same conclusion.

In his commentary on the passage in the *Book of Enunciation*, he says, " Et non dividuntur enunciationes ex parte conjunctionis clausuræ cum prædicato; quia, clausura cum *adjungitur prædicato*, est *falsa* enunciatio, aut *superflua*; et falsa quidem est, ' omnis homo est omne animal ;' superflua sicut cum diximus, ' *omnis homo est quoddam animal.*' " (*Averrois Opera omnia.* Venet. 1560. Tom. i. fol. 45.) He has another sentence to the same effect in his commentary on the twenty-seventh chapter of the first book of the *Prior Analytics*. It is as follows—" Oportet ut sepimentum (hoc est determinatio) semper coaptetur subjecto propositionis acceptæ, *non autem prædicato*, quoniam si conjungetur prædicato, erit aut *impossibilis*, aut *inutilis* ad syllogismum, secundum quod declaratum fuit in libro præcedente." Fol. 118.

The first of these extracts from Averroes, though so brief, is curious, inasmuch as he there explicitly takes account of what is not noticed by Aristotle or Boëthius before him, or, as far as I remember, by any of the rejectors of a quantified predicate after him,—the case, to wit, in which the predicate is quantified *particularly*. He considers, with Aristotle, first, the case in which it is quantified *universally*, " all man is all animal," and, with him, rejects this as false and impossible. He then proceeds to consider the case in which it is quantified *particularly*, " all man is *some* animal;" here he was free to act as he would, for of this second case nothing had been said; but the spell of Aristotle's rejection of the universal quantification was still strong upon him, and accordingly he rejects the *particular* also as *superfluous* and *useless*. The grounds of this rejection are, it need scarcely be said, totally extra-logical; for the particular quantification of the predicate in the given example is *superfluous* only by an appeal to the *matter of the proposition*, with which logic has nothing whatever to do; and so far from being *useless*, such quantification is *absolutely necessary*, before the predicate notion, as the constituent of a reasoning, can be turned to its full scientific account.

From Boëthius and Averroes, the logical treatises of Aristotle, with the traditions founded upon them, passed, as we have said, to the schoolmen; among these Albertus Magnus and St. Thomas Aquinas are quoted as having anew defended the rejection of a quantified predicate. The hereditary confession of logical faith, now become venerable through constant subscription, passed from the schoolmen to the later commentators on the Organon. These, while throwing off, to a great extent, the formality of the scholastic style, are yet rarely wise in important points above the teaching of their masters. On the point in question, that of a quantified predicate, they seem to have remained, with scarcely an exception, faithful to the received traditions. In illustration of this we will take two, which are among the best and most valuable of the later commentaries on the Organon, that of *Julius Pacius*, and that of the *College of the Society of Jesus at Coimbra*.

Julius Pacius, the pupil of Zabarella, and preceptor in philosophy of Casaubon, was both a very learned and a very acute man; and his works accordingly exhibit the accuracy and penetration resulting from these blended excellencies. His commentary on the Organon was first published in the year 1597. It was so full, clear, and precise, and altogether such a useful book, that it speedily attained a high reputation, and has ever since maintained its place as a standard work on the Organon. Pacius discusses the question of a quantified predicate in connexion with both the passages which we have quoted from the Organon; and as his opinion in this matter stands in much the same relation to the later philosophy as that of Boëthius did to the earlier, it may be worth while to quote it in full. The more so, too, as it is in itself the fullest discussion of the matter probably to be found among the later writers.

The first passage is from his Commentary on the *Book of Enunciation;* it is as follows :—

" In duabus primis particulis sejunxerat indefinitas ab universalibus ; quoniam universales subjecto universali addunt notam universalem *omnis*, vel *nullus ;* indefinitæ verò nullam notam subjecto apponunt. Unde potuisset aliquis suspicari tale discrimen, quod modò exposuimus in subjecto, nempe recipere notam universalem, aut eâ notâ carere, tale (inquam) discrimen etiam in attributo spectari posse ; quasi vel simpliciter proponi possit, vel cum nota universali. Hunc errorem ut Aristoteles tollat, ostendit *universalem notam nunquam posse adjungi attributo :* quia tunc omnis affirmatio *falsa* esset.

Quod declarat exemplo hujus enunciationis, 'omnis homo est omne animal,' quæ sine dubio falsa est: nam si homo esset omne animal, esset etiam asinus et bos. Sed notare hic oportet, alia attributa latius patere quam subjecta, alia verò reciprocari cum subjectis. Hoc est quod dicebat Porphyrius, cap. 2, pars 37, aut majora de minoribus aut æqualia de æqualibus dici. Ubi igitur attributum latius patet, ut in exemplo Aristotelis, res dubitatione caret: certum enim est, affirmationem esse falsam, nec posse dici, 'omnem hominem esse omne animal.' Sed meritò dubitatur de attributis, quæ reciprocantur cum subjectis, veluti si quis dicat, 'omne animal est omne sensu præditum,' et 'omnis homo est omne aptum ad ridendum :' nam hic absurditas illa non æquè apparet, ut in illa enunciatione, 'omnis homo est omne animal.' Sed ut intelligatur has quoque enunciationes esse falsas, in quibus attributum, quod reciprocatur, adnexam habet particulam *omnis*, notare oportet, hanc particulam *omnis*, habere vim quam in scholis vocant distributivam; ut omnis homo, proinde valeat atque quilibet homo, vel *singuli homines;* et similiter omne animal, idem valet, quod singula animalia, vel unumquodque animal seu quodlibet animal. Quapropter si verè diceretur, 'omne animal est omne sensu præditum,' etiam homo esset omne sensu præditum; nam qui dixit omne animal, non exclusit omnem hominem, homo igitur esset quodlibet sensu præditum: proinde hac ratione fieret, ut homo esset equus, et bos, quandoquidem equus et bos sunt sensu prædita." (*Pacius in Aristotelis De Interpret.* cap. vii.)

The second passage is from the commentary on the *Prior Analytics,* and is as follows :—

" Quintum præceptum est, ne sumamus consequens, quod totam consequatur, sed quod toti sit consequens : id est, ut nota universalis *omnis* vel *omne*, jungatur subjecto, non attributo propositionis. Primò, Aristoteles proponit hoc præceptum. Deinde, cum ait, 'verbi gratiâ,' præceptum illud exemplis illustrat. Tertiò, cum ait, 'quonium alterum,' duplici argumento præceptum illud confirmat. Primum est; quia si sumas id, quod totum consequitur, pars ejus erit inutilis, et ad rem non faciat. Alterum argumentum est; quia propositio erit impossibilis, id est, necessario falsa. Posterius argumentum declarat his exemplis, ' omnis homo est omne animal,' et ' justitia est omne bonum.' Nam hæ propositiones sunt evidenter falsæ, ut etiam expositum fuit *Capite* 7, *De Interp. Partic.* 4. Prius argumentum ab Aristotele non explicatur, ideoque a nobis est breviter explicandum. Ergo etiamsi verè dici possit, omnem hominem est omne animal; tamen illud *omne* nihil faceret ad concludendum problema; tantumdem enim valet hæc propositio, ' omnis homo est animal.' Exempli gratiâ, si probandum sit, omnem hominem, vivere; et primum, sumatur hæc propositio, ' omne animal vivit;' si addas assumptionem, quod ' omnis homo est animal,' etiamsi non sumas esse omne animal, tamen rectè colliges omnem hominem vivere. Postremo, cum ait, ' sed cui [aliud]' concludit universalem illam notam *omnis*, esse subjecto adjungendam." (*Pacius in Arist. Analyt. Pri.* i. cap. 27, § 9.)

The commentary on the Organon by the *College of Coimbra* was first published in the year 1600, a few years after that of Pacius. It was one of those able works on philosophy to which, after the decline of scholasticism, the zeal and energy of the Jesuits in letters and philosophy gave birth. It is far from being a mere slavish transcript from previous writers, but has on the contrary acuteness and originality enough to enable it to stand out in its individuality from the works of the time. In relation to the point in question it is, however, in harmony with its predecessors and contemporaries. The following is its deliverance on the matter:—

"Docuerat (Aristoteles) in propositionibus universalibus signa universalia addi subjecto, ambigeret quis, an prædicato etiam addi oporteret, ut quemadmodum dicimus, ' omnis homo est animal,' libeat ita loqui, ' omnis homo est omne animal:' respondet negativè in affirmativis, quia aliter *omnis affirmatio uni-*

versalis falsa esset, veluti si dicas, ' omnis homo est omne animal,'
neque enim omne animal in homine est. Notanter, addit Aristoteles, nulla erit affirmatio vera, quia in quavis materia, etsi
prædicatum æquale existat *subjecto,* propositio erit *falsa.* Nam
sensus hujus propositionis, ' omnis homo est omne risible,' est
quod *hic* homo est omne risible, et *ille* homo est omne risible,
distribuit enim particula *omnis,* subjectum copulativè pro omnibus. Unde patet, quam errent Averroes et Boëthius existi-
mantes addi posse signum universale prædicato, universalis propositionis, quando illud exæquat subjectum : nisi propositionis
accipiant non copulativè præter earum usum et naturam. De
negativa propositione nihil docet quia in ea, etsi negatio addi
possit prædicato absque falsitate, superflua tamen est, quia vir-
tute præcedentis negationis ad omnia extenditur prædicatum."
(*Comment. Coll. Conimbr. in universam Dialecticam Aristotelis.*
Colon., 1611. Pars ii. p. 158.)

I confess that Boëthius and Averroes appear to me to be but
hardly treated in the above passage, in being held guilty of error
for saying that the universal quantification of the predicate,
when it was equal in extent to the subject, was simply superfluous, instead of denouncing it as false. Boëthius, indeed, as
we have seen, hypothetically does the latter, but considers the
whole case with far greater wisdom than his censor, since he
says in relation to it, that the quantification is *superfluous,* if the
subject be taken *collectively,* but *false* if it be taken *distributively.*
With the exception of the admission that the predicate of a
negative judgment may be quantified, without making the
proposition false, the above extract is at one with the previous
authorities.

Keckermann adds nothing new, save one example, (which is,
however, something, where the whole question is solved by
examples,) if possible, still more inept, not to say absurd,
than the common ones. A number of other logical writers,
about equal in authority to Keckermann, such as Burgersdyk,

Hereboord, Stahl,* Derodon, &c., might be referred to as giving
deliverances to the same effect. There is nothing, however, in
their statement of the common opinion that merits special attention, or that need be quoted here.

Such is the position which the opinion of the illegality of
quantification in relation to the predicate has maintained in the
history of the science. It has been held from the earliest to the
latest times. Nor is it by any means yet obsolete. With the
exception of the comparatively few quarters in which Sir W.
Hamilton's refutation of the old, and application of the new doctrine, have become known, it is as firmly and as widely held to-
day as it ever was. The marvellous acuteness of Kant, in relation to everything connected with formal thought, which did
good service in other parts of logic, brought no help here. Nor
has the newly-kindled zeal on behalf of Aristotle and his philosophy, manifested in Germany and France, been of any more
avail. The last German editor of the Organon, Theo. Waitz,
still says, on the classical passage in the Book of Enunciation,—
" Quum additur ' omnis,' non id de quo prædicatur universale esse significatur, sed de re aliqua universa aliquid prædicari judicatur. Si vero quod prædicatur, quum universale est, universum prædicatur, *enunciatio exit non vera.*"—
(*Aristotelis Organon, Edidit T. Waitz.* 1844. Pars i. p. 337.)
Finally, the last French translator and expositor of Aristotle, M.
J. B. Saint-Hilaire, in his excellent version of the Organon,

* Stahl and Derodon have been quoted already in the Essay. While
referring again to Stahl, I may mention here what ought to have been
stated in the note respecting him at page 2, viz., that in what he says of
comprehension and *extension*, he but repeats Cajetanus, quoted, indeed, himself to the same effect earlier in his work. (*Reg. Phil.*, p. 381.) The work of
Cajetanus on the categories from which Stahl quotes, dates from 1496, so
that the discrimination of these quantities by the epithets *extensive* and *intensive* is of some antiquity. The term *intensive* was commonly employed
in the Leibnitian school in the same sense, and was probably revived by
Leibnitz, immediately from Cajetanus, or mediately through Stahl.

still reiterates, without a reason, in his notes, the rejection of the text:—" L'attribut n'a jamais la marque d'universalité : et l'on ne saurait dire : Tout homme est *tout* animal : on dit simple-ment et d'une manière absolue : Tout homme est animal. Le signe d'universalité n'est jamais qu' à l'antécédent, c'est-à-dire, au sujèt."—(*Logique d'Aristote, trad.* Paris, 1839. Tom. ii. p. 125.)

To sum up, then, the evidence we have obtained, the whole question, as commonly treated by the logicians, may be stated as follows :—The predicate, they consider, (with a single excep-tion,) can only be quantified *universally*. Now, this being the only possibility contemplated, two cases arise ; for either, in the *first place*, the predicate is *greater* than the subject, and then such quantification is *false*, as "all man is all animal;" or it is *equal* to the subject, and then such quantification is *superfluous*, as " all man is all risible." The later commentators, however, are not satisfied with this comparatively mild dismissal of the second case, but maintain, that in *any case*, in the latter as well as in the former, the quantification is necessarily *false ;* and this on the apparently inconceivably inconsequent ground, that if *all man* is all risible, then necessarily *each man* is all risible ; or to take a parallel example, (one, however, which they do not take,) that if *twelve inches* are one foot, then necessarily *each individual inch* is also one foot.

When we consider these grounds, and remember the real ability of the men by whom they were successively urged, we cannot but be struck with a wonder amounting to marvel, that they could remain satisfied with them, and that a truth so obvious on its first enunciation, so imperative on its fuller exposition, should have been so uniformly and so long thus rejected. Allow-ing that the original judgment of Aristotle was given rashly upon but a partial consideration of the subject, we still cannot at all understand how his followers should not, on the one hand, having undertaken its examination, have discovered its fallacy, or, on the other, having adopted and undertaken to defend it, have offered something better—something at least not absurd—in its vindication. It is, however, but another instance, perhaps the most illustrious of all, of what has been often noticed, of how completely the weight of authority often prevails against the clearest evidence. As in physical science the older philosophers refused to believe the evidence of their senses against the recorded judgment of Aristotle, so in mental science they refused to accept the equally obvious evidence of their understandings, where it testified against the same infallible authority.

The only explanation which can be offered of this strange oversight, and it is probably the true one, is, that the logicians for the most part (after Aristotle) limited their attention to the single case of universal quantification. This, considered in relation to the rules which were already laid down for predication, according to which the predicate notion was always of greater extent than the subject notion, would not only naturally, but necessarily lead to the rejection of such one-sided quantification.

Some exceptions do, however, as we have said, occur, in which the subject is looked at in a wider aspect, and to these it is time that we should more explicitly refer.

II. *Some exceptions to the common doctrine, in which the principle of a quantified predicate receives a more enlightened consideration, and is partially, either in principle or practice, formally allowed.*

Laurentius Valla was, so far as I know, the first by whom the express quantification of the predicate was in any form, or to any extent allowed. And if, indeed, the force of the tradition against it was ever to be broken through, this was a service which we might naturally have expected to receive at his hands, since he was assuredly one of the most independent and active thinkers, not alone of his own, but also of any age. The same originality of which his life and writings were the constant expression, characterises also his logical inquiries. He complained of the diffuseness and defects of the existing logic, undertook a thorough examination of its doctrines, and accepted none but such as appeared founded on the truth of things. Whatever, therefore, rested simply on authority he at once threw aside, while whatever appeared to have scientific evidence in its favour he with equal readiness adopted. As the result of this thorough independence, he was doubtless sometimes led into error, from which an adherence to authority would have preserved him; but he was often also led into truth, to which the force of authority would as certainly have denied his access; so that on the whole he certainly introduced more truth than error into the science, and had he been less hasty and capricious, the result of his labours would probably have been still more valuable. As it is, however, his treatise has all the freshness and vigour of independent thought, and with no loss of accuracy, possesses the rare merit of being a really interesting introduction to a science not proverbial for the attractiveness of its elementary works.

Valla flourished during the first half of the fifteenth century, having been born at Rome in 1408, and dying in 1457. His logical work, *De Dialectica*, dates therefore from the middle of that century. I cannot find, however, any account of a printed edition of it before the one published at Venice in the year 1499, though in all probability it must have been printed much earlier. From the title of this earlier edition, " *De Dialectica contra Aristoteleos,*" it would seem at first to have been avowedly published against the logicians of the day; as it is quite certain, from his short defence of himself at the close of the work, that Valla did not escape severe censure, and indeed persecution. The boldness of his criticisms on the current doctrines, indeed, (though these were coupled for the most part with the most respectful references to Aristotle himself,) when taken in connexion with the enmity aroused by his stubborn adherence to the truths which he had obtained by his own industry, and his contemptuous rejection of those which were merely traditional;—his criticisms, we say, taken in connexion with the enmity which his conduct in these respects had excited, were likely enough to provoke active and fierce opposition. His attack (or what seemed an attack) upon the time-honoured and sacred fortress of the Aristotelic logic, would naturally be the signal for a general assault on the part of his enemies. There are none, however, but must be struck with the calm beauty and dignity of his protest against the meanness and the malice of the persecutions to which he had been subjected for his defence of what he held to be the truth; and none, too, however wayward, haughty, and petulant that defence may sometimes have been, who will not heartily respond to the noble sentiment with which he closes:—" Verum Imperator noster, Deus, milites suos ex acie fugere non vult ; sed aut vincere, aut strenue fortiterque pugnantes, mortem oppetere. Non enim ipsis pereuntibus veritatis gloria perit, sed vivit, sed vincit, sed illo piissimo cruore sancitur, atque consecratur." For myself I feel that I could freely forgive the errors of his life had they been far more serious than they were, when I find him consciously upheld by such high inspiration; and see that amidst all its pride and storm he cherished so sincere a love for the truth, and so stern a determination to defend it, against all odds, and at every hazard.

Some apology, we feel, is due for having dwelt so long upon the man, when it is, in strictness of speech, with his doctrine that we are here alone concerned. We trust that this may be found in the fact, that he is at once the least known, and the best worth knowing of all logical writers. To return, however, to his work,—the only edition of this with which I am acquainted is that printed at Paris in the year 1530, 4to, and it is from this accordingly that I uniformly quote. This edition has not the title given above, but simply the following,—" *Laurentii*

Vallœ Romani De Dialectica, libri iii." In this work, as we have
said, Valla allows the express quantification of the predicate in
theory, and to a certain, but very limited extent, adopts it in practice. Before, however, referring to the passages* which contain
the evidence of this, it may be worth while to look for a moment
at what he says of *Conversion.* This is very curious and acute;
and though it does not explicitly bring out his doctrine of the predicate, will yet very well serve as introductory thereto. In his
chapter, " *De Convertenda Enunciatione,*" he says as follows :—

" Hic locus admonet ut aliqua de conversione dicamus : nam
licet major atque amplior significatio prædicati fere sit quam
subjecti, sicut ostendi; non tamen amplius ac latius *accipitur
prædicatum* quam subjectum. Ideoque cum illo converti potest,
ut ' omnis homo est animal,' non utique *totum genus* animal, sed
aliqua pars hujus generis; nam Cicero speciem partem generis
vocat; *ergo aliqua pars animalis est in omni homine.* Item ' quidam
homo est animal,' scilicet est *quædam pars animalis;* ergo ' quædam pars animalis est quidam homo.' ' Omnis leo est rutilis,'
' quidam leo est rutilis;' hoc est, quod quisque leo, et quidam
leo partem aliquam habet sive quandam rutili coloris, non ipsum
omnino rutilum colorem; ergo *aliqua pars rutili coloris* est in
singulis leonibus, et quædam in quodam. Idem intelligo de in-
finito quod de universali, cum universaliter accipitur. Idem
quoque de particulari singularique, cum particulariter singu-
lariterque significat: nec aliter, cum totaliter accipitur, ut
' homo est *species* animalis,' id est *quædam species* animalis ; ergo
' *quædam animalis species est homo.*' In negatione ratio e diverso
est, quando adest signum universale; ut ' nullus homo est
satyrus,' id est ' nullus homo non [?] est ullus satyrus;' ergo

* I may state at once that I do not profess to give *all* the references to
this subject which may be found in Valla. I give only the passages which
I marked in a former reading, undertaken without express reference to
the doctrine of the predicate. The urgency of the press is too great to allow of my going through it carefully again with this end specially in view.

' nullus satyrus non [?] est ullus homo.'   Quando non adest, ut
' homo non est satyrus,' id est, ' *ullus homo,*' ' *ullus satyrus ;*' ergo,
' ullus satyrus non est ullus homo.'   Quando per totalitatem
loquimur, ut ' satyrus non est *species* hominis,' id est, ' *ulla species*
hominis,' ergo ' *ulla species hominis non est satyrus.*'   Quando
adest signum particulare singulareve, ut ' nonnullus piscis,' vel
' hic piscis fœtum enititur,' scilicet est aliquis ex illis piscibus qui
fœtum enituntur; ergo aliquis ex piscibus fœtum enitentibus
est aliquis, vel est hic.   Item, ' ille piscis' vel ' hic piscis non est
fœtum enitens, sed ova pariens ;' videlicet ex iis qui fœtum enituntur, ergo aliquis piscis ex iis qui fœtum enituntur, sed ova
non pariunt, non est ille, vel non est hic piscis.   ' Thales est
unus ex septem sapientibus,' id est *aliquis* ex septem, ergo ' aliquis ex septem Thales.'   ' Pythagoras non fuit e septem sapientibus,' id est *ullus* e septem, ergo ' ullus e septem non fuit
Pythagoras.' "—*De Dialectica,* fol. 37.

Valla has here manifestly penetrated into the true nature of
conversion.   His doctrine, in effect, is, that by explicating the
proposition, the conversion is, in any case, a simple turning of
the sentence.   Thus, for example, when we say, " all man is
animal," what do we mean ?   Obviously, that all man is *some*
animal, or *a species* of animal, or *a certain species* of animal;
therefore, " a certain species of animal is all man."   In other
words, that though the predicate notion is in general, absolutely
considered, of wider extent than the subject notion, yet that
when considered relatively in a proposition, its extent is always
restricted to that of the notion with which it is connected; so
that by expressing this restriction, that is, by explicating the
proposition, the subject and predicate are always convertible
terms, and thus all conversion is necessarily *simple.*   He accomplishes this, it will be seen, by explicitly quantifying the predicate ; as, no man is a satyr—that is, *any satyr.*   He has, however, blundered in the example.   He should have given *ullus*
for *nullus,* or *est* for *non est.*

We pass on, however, to his more explicit judgment in this matter. In the third book of his Treatise, Valla considers the right of the predicate to the marks of quantification in a brief chapter devoted expressly to this subject. It is headed, " *Dum signum applicatur prædicato, dumque abest a toto syllogismo signum,*" and is as follows :—" Hactenus locuti sumus cum signum universale applicatur *subjecto:* quid cum applicatur *prædicato ?* Certe pari ratione ; quæ exempla breviter subnectam, ' Tu amas *omnes* tuos cives, hi autem *omnes* sunt cives tui, ergo, tu amas hos *omnes.*' Hoc universaliter ; particulariter vero si assumas, ' hic est civis tuus,' concludasque ' ergo, tu amas *hunc ;*' sive diverso exemplo, ' Deus est ubique,' id est in *omni loco,* ' Tartarus est locus, ergo Deus est in Tartaro.' Hoc affirmative ; negative sic, ' tu nullum civem tuum, sive nullos cives tuos amas, hi omnes sunt cives tui, ergo *neminem* vel *nullum* horum amas.' Item, ' in nullo loco scelerato est Deus, Tartarus talis est, ergo non est in eo Deus.' Exempla quæ attuli per signa universalia, si tollamus signa, *eandem vim* habebunt redacta ad infinita, ut superiore libro probavi ; ut, Deus non est in loco scelerato, sive in locis sceleratis, *subauditur* enim *ullo,* sive *ullis ;* tu non amas cives tuos, *subintelligitur omnes.* Idem fit in superioribus exemplis, ac cæteris omnibus."—Cap. xlvii. fol. 62.

Here the quantification of the predicate is explicitly allowed ; and though the examples given of its lawfulness be incorrect, the rules of the common doctrine are falsified. For these examples are *affirmative* syllogisms of the *second* figure, contrary to the law that all valid reasonings in that figure must be *negative.* It is also further shown in this chapter that the quantity of the predicate is invariably a *determinate* one, and that when not so expressed, it is nevertheless always understood.

Valla here accordingly allows the quantification in theory, elsewhere he follows it in practice. Besides the examples given above, I remember two other passages in which he does this.

The first is, when speaking of *subcontraries,* he employs the express quantification to prove that these cannot both be false. The passage is as follows :—

" Quocirca propria et pene sola subcontrarietas est in pronominibus ac propriis nominibus, nunquam (ut dixi) utraque parte vera. Quo magis illorum confutatur opinio, quibus placuit duas aliquando subcontrarias simul esse falsas, *ubi eorum prædicatis adest signum universale ;* ut ' Plato est *omne* animal,' ' Plato est *nullum* animal.' Neque enim sunt veræ subcontrariæ quarum secunda non negat quod prior affirmat. Habet itaque illa affirmativa, ' Plato est omne animal,' suam negativam, ' Plato non est omne animal;' et hæc negativa suam affirmativam, 'Plato est *aliquod* animal,' quia *ullum* dicere non possumus."—Cap. xxxv. fol. 48. The whole passage is longer, and the quantified predicate is used in illustration of the same point to the end of the chapter; but the above extract may suffice to illustrate this use.

The second passage is contained in a brief but important chapter, headed, " *Syllogismi per totum et partem.*" The two last sentences contain the specific examples, but the whole chapter is well worth quoting, and the more so, since in some of the earlier examples also the predicate is quantified. It is as follows :—

" Similis ratio in* toto et parte, quæ in genere et specie ; quæ

---

* Valla seems somewhat strangely to employ the terms *whole* and *part*, exclusively in relation to *physical wholes and parts*. In this chapter, accordingly, under the general head of whole and part, he confines his attention entirely to these, without making any reference to the wholes and parts which had been commonly discriminated as *logical* and *metaphysical*. To the *logical* or *extensive* whole, indeed, no express reference was necessary, since all ordinary syllogistic reasonings (his own amongst the rest) proceeded in this quantity, it being the only one formally recognised in the science. To the metaphysical whole he himself refers elsewhere. In a previous chapter, devoted to the consideration of the *order of the syllogistic parts*, he gives an example of a reasoning in the metaphysical or comprehensive whole, and very sagaciously asks, why the syllogism does not proceed in this order, from the individual or species to the genus—from the narrower to the wider notion ? " What is the reason," says he, " that we may not construct a syllogism thus—' Socrates is man ; but all man is

exempla brevissime subjungam. Prima forma erit hæc, 'Tota Italia est in Europa; tota Campania est in Italia; ergo tota Campania est in Europa.' Altera quæ hujus particularis est, hæc erit, 'Tota Campania est in Italia; Neapolis est *pars* Campaniæ; ergo est in Italia.' Tertia, negativa, hæc, 'nihil Italiæ est in Asia; tota Campania est in Italia; ergo nihil Campaniæ est in Asia.' Quarta quæ hujus particularis est, hæc, ' Nihil Ægypti est in Africa; Alexandria est *aliquid* Ægypti; sive *pars* sive *pars quædam* Ægypti; ergo non est in Africa.' Nam 'nihil,' idem est quod 'non aliquid,' sive ' non quiddam,' id est non ulla res, sive non quædam res, quemadmodum superius docui; sicut ' omne' et ' omnia' substantivum, id est omnis vel omnes res.

" Quando *adest prædicato signum*, hæc quoque sint exempla; ' *totum* corpus anima nutrit; toti ungues sunt *pars* corporis; ergo *totcs* ungues anima nutrit.' Vel assumendo particulariter, quæ est secunda forma; ' hic unguis est *pars* corporis; ergo *hunc* unguem anima nutrit.'

" Item negative : ' Nihil corporis anima negligit; toti ungues sunt *aliquid*, vel *pars* corporis, sive hic unguis est *aliquid*, vel *pars quædam* corporis; ergo nihil unguium, aut non hunc unguem anima negligit."—Cap. xlix. fol. 62.

It will be seen that in these last examples the rules of the common doctrine are again falsified; for they contain syllogisms of the second figure, some of which are affirmative, and others particular. The examples may, indeed, be objected to.

Such is the doctrine of Laurentius Valla on the point in question; and it will be seen from the extracts we have given, that he recognises (though appreciating very partially and imperfectly its significance) the express quantification of the predicate.

animal, therefore Socrates is animal;' ascending as it were by certain steps, Socrates the individual, man the species, animal the genus?" This was in effect asking, though he himself probably did not see the full meaning of his own question, why the syllogism in logic did not proceed in the whole of *comprehension* as well as in that of *extension ;* a wise question, which was not replied to, by subsequent logicians, and remains still unanswered.

The two next witnesses whose evidence I have to quote in
favour of a quantified predicate, have this much in common—
that they were contemporaries—were both men of great learning and ability—both acute writers on logic—both well and
widely known in their own day, and that their names and works
have long since passed into utter forgetfulness. It may, I believe, be added, that I am the first in modern times to have
directed any attention to their writings;—they are Jodocus T.
Isenach of Erfurt, and Ambrosius Leo of Venice. Of these we
shall take the latter first, since, as a fellow-countryman, his
evidence will naturally enough follow that of Laurentius Valla.

Ambrosius Leo* was a physician at Venice, and flourished

* Ambrosius Leo, called from Nola the place of his birth *Nolanus*, was
one of that noble band of men, distinguished for varied genius and scholar-
ship, whose labours towards the close of the fifteenth, and commencement
of the sixteenth centuries, conferred on Venice a name of imperishable re-
nown. He was, as stated in the text, for many years a physician in that
city, but like several of his craft at that time, was not only skilled in medi-
cine as a physician, but also profound as a philosopher, erudite as a scholar,
and accomplished in all worthy and noble arts as a gentleman. His very
name, however, seems to have been long since forgotten, and his works to
have passed into complete oblivion. For a time, indeed, these seem to have
been kept in some remembrance, since they appear in some of the older
catalogues of distinguished works and authors. Thus, Simler, in his epitome
of the Bibliotheca of Conrad Gesner, says, " *Ambrosius Leo* Nolanus scripsit
opus quæstionum, tum aliis plerisque in rebus cognoscendis, tum maxime
in philosophia et medicinæ scientia. Impressum Venetiis 1523. Idem edidit Castigationes in Averroem, qui liber magnus est, ac totius philosophiæ
thesaurus. Sunt enim quasi commentarii quidam, ordine in singulos Aristotelis libros. Excusæ Venetiis 1517. Actuarii Johannis Zachariæ filii de
urinis libros septem, ex Græcis Latinos fecit. Impressi Basileæ apud Cra-
tandrum 1528."—(*Epitome Bibliothecæ Conradi Gesneri per Josiam Sim-
lerum. Tiguri* 1555.)

And Vossius adds to this comment the following :—" Anno 1517, ac
deinceps, non exiguæ eruditionis laudem reportavit Ambrosius Leo Nolanus, vir Latine Græceque doctissimus, philosophus idem, ac medicus in-
signis. Hic præter ea, quæ a Simlero memorantur, reliquit libros tres de
Nola non incuriosè perscriptos : quorum sæpius meminit Leander Albertus
in descriptione Italiæ : imprimis quo loco agit de Nola."—(*De Hist. Lat.*
L. iii. c. xii.)

He appears to have soon lost even such distinction as this, for his name

during the latter part of the fifteenth and the beginning of
the sixteenth century. He was the author of several smaller
treatises, but his greatest production is a work against Averroes,

does not appear in any of the later catalogues of a similar kind which I
have been able to examine. Indeed, for some time after having obtained
his work against Averroes, I could not find out who or what he was. At
length, however, I discovered that he was a friend of Erasmus, the latter
having become known to Leo during his stay in Venice, and having afterwards corresponded with him. In the Epistles of Erasmus, accordingly,
there are a few scattered references to Ambrosius Leo, and to this source
I am mainly indebted for the few particulars of his history with which I
am acquainted.

The first mention of Leo which we meet with in the Epistles, is in a letter
written to Erasmus by John Watson, and dated from Cambridge in the
month of August 1515. Speaking of a recent visit to Venice, Watson says,
" I conversed almost daily with the physician Ambrosius Leo in the apo-
thecary's shop at the sign of the Coral. I remembered him from what you
had said of him, in connexion with the proverb, δὶς διὰ πασῶν. He did
many things for me, for your sake." The reference here is to the " Adagia"
of Erasmus, who, in his commentary on the proverb quoted above, refers to
Ambrosius Leo in the following manner :—" Etenim cum hæc meis illinirem
commentariis, forte fortuna supervenit Ambrosius. Leo Nolanus philosophus hujus tempestatis eximius, et in pervestigandis disciplinarum mys-
teriis incredibili quadam diligentia solertiaque præditus; neque vero medio-
criter exercitatus evolvendis et excutiendis utriusque linguæ scriptoribus."
—(*Adagia Erasmi*, in h. l.)

In the summer of the year 1518, Leo himself writes to Erasmus, and after
referring to a small work which he had written on the history of his native
town and district, Nola, and to other labours in which he had been engaged,
tells him that he has completed a great work, divided into forty-six books,
peripatetic in doctrine, and written against Averroes. Erasmus writes a long
and very interesting letter in reply, almost a twelvemonth afterwards, in
which he calls to remembrance the pleasant intercourse he had had with
Leo and his brother scholars at Venice, and congratulates him upon the
happy fortune which had cast his lot among the most learned scholars
and in the first city of the world :—" Quo minus expectatæ venerunt tuæ
literæ, *Ambrosi* doctissime, hoc mihi plus voluptatis attulerunt. Sic enim
mihi totam illam nostræ consuetudinis memoriam renovarunt, ut eas legens
apud *Venetos* mihi viderer agere, veteres amicos meos tueri coram et am-
plecti, *Aldum, Baptistam Egnatium, Hieronymum Aleandrum, M. Musu-
rum,* te cum primis amicorum omnium suavissimum. Agnosco lepidissimos
tuos mores in epistola tua, quæ tota jocis ac salibus scatet. O te felicem,
cui contigerit in pulcherrimis studiis, et in urbe facile omnium magnificen-
tissima, inter patricios et eruditos viros consenescere !"

entitled "*Ambrosii Nolani Castigationes, adversus Averroem*."
This was first published at Venice in the year 1517, and again
at the same place in 1532. The first part of the work is occu-

He afterwards expresses his earnest wish that the book against Averroes
were published.

We hear no more of Leo in the Epistles till the year 1528, in which year
he seems to have died, for in the month of October in that year, Erasmus
writing to a friend, says :—"*Ambrosium Nolanum* nobis ac studiis ereptum
doleo, sed quandoquidem omnibus semel est moriendum, ille nec vixit in-
commode multos annos, nec infeliciter mortuus est."—(*Opera omnia Erasmi.
Ed. Clerici.* Lugd. Vol. iii., pp. 161, 334, 506, 594.)

The most considerable of the works of Ambrosius Leo, both in value and
extent, is evidently this one against Averroes. It is a large folio volume,
containing upwards of 1100 pages ; and comprises within itself, as Simler
says, a perfect storehouse of philosophy. He follows Averroes pertina-
ciously into almost all subjects, and seems equally at home in logical, mathematical, physical, or metaphysical discussions. I speak, of course, only from
a limited knowledge of the work, having only consulted it in relation to
particular subjects in which I felt specially interested; but the acuteness
and knowledge it displays seem equally balanced and both great. The
reading of Leo, indeed, appears to have been not only very extensive, but
critical and exact; he is critically read (as were all the learned men of his
time) in ancient Greek philosophy; and what was a less common accom-
plishment, seems also quite familiar with all the later Greek and Latin commentators. The wide reading and varied sagacity which it displays, as well
as the size of the work itself, are quite sufficient to explain the declaration
he playfully makes in writing to Erasmus, that he did not waste away his
nights in bed.

This volume is, as I have said, now of the greatest rarity. The biogra-
phers of Averroes, as far as I can find, are ignorant of its existence. The
ordinary bibliographers make no reference to it. It is not, so far as I can
ascertain, in any of the public libraries of the country. And what, perhaps, is a stronger proof of its rarity than anything else, and proves it to
be as little known on the continent as in this country, is the fact, that a
man so curiously and widely read as Morhof, should not only never
have seen it, but expresses his belief that it was never published. In his
Polyhistor, Morhof, while referring to the notices in the letters of Erasmus
that such a work was in preparation, says, at the same time, that he does
not believe that it was ever really published.

In abatement, however, of the statement, as to the utter oblivion into
which the name of Ambrosius Leo has fallen, I should say that it is still
remembered in connexion with his small work on the history of Nola, which
is not very rare, and is still, I see, referred to in connexion with the history
of the Italian states.

pied with a detailed criticism of the commentary of Averroes
on the Organon; and in this he examines, among other state-
ments, what Averroes says on the passage in the book touching
enunciation relative to the quantification of the predicate. We
have already given the passage from Averroes. Leo joins issue
with him on this statement; he takes the case which is also
taken by Averroes, but not referred to by Aristotle,—that in
which the predicate is quantified particularly,—and he defends
against Averroes the validity and usefulness of such quantification. The passage in which he does this is a somewhat long
one; but as the rarity of the work is such as to preclude anything like general reference, it may be worth while to give it
entire. It ought to be premised, however, that the text is in
such a state, partly through carelessness in printing, partly
through excessive and strange contraction, that the making it
out, in many cases, is a kind of divination. It is as follows :—

" Aliud est non recipere *rem*, et aliud non recipere *divisionem
rei;* ut aliud est non recipere esse genus, id quod dicimus pe-
destre, et aliud non recipere divisionem pedestris in bipes et
multipes; unde Aristoteles genera facillime recipit, divisiones
vero eorum facile non recipit. Non igitur, si enunciationes quæ
in prædicato habent clausuram non dividuntur, etiam non recipiuntur, nam existere possunt etiam sine divisione; sed potius si
non recipiuntur, non etiam dividuntur : quamobrem Aristoteles
monet non esse recipiendas, non autem non esse dividendas.
Idem aptius in primo Priorum docuit. ' Ut similiter,' inquit, ' eli-
gendum, et quæ ipsum sequitur tota, per eandem causam; ipsum
autem quod sequitur, non esse sumendum totum sequi. Dico
autem, ut *in homine esse omne animal,* aut *in musica omnem dis-
ciplinam;* sed tamen simpliciter sequi, quemadmodum antea
monuimus. Etenim inutile alterum et impossibile, ut *omnem
hominem esse omne animal,* vel *omnem justitiam omne bonum;* sed
cui alterum consequens est, in illo *omne* dicitur.' Hæc ille. Quare
ab arte repelluntur tales propositiones ut ineptæ et malæ; non

autem non numerantur, vel dividuntur, propter eas causas : nam
hac via qua ivit Averroes, non excludere moneremur, quas excludere velle ars ipsa comperitur. Quinetiam ubi legisset Averroes hæc Aristotelis verba : ' Sed universale prædicatum universaliter prædicare, non est verum ; nulla enim affirmatio vera
erit, in qua prædicatum fuerit universaliter universale, ut, *est
omnis homo omne animal:*' vidissetque *nihil dictum esse ab Aristotele de nota particularitatis,* quonam modo se haberet, si etiam
prædicato termino addita fuisset. Voluit eum locum, veluti
mancum, exponendo perficere ; dicens de *omni clausura,* ut
si universalis clausura est addita prædicato, enunciatio erit
falsa, si particularis, erit superflua. Aristoteles vero, neque
hic, neque in loco *Priorum* prædicto, meminit particularitatis,
atque superfluitatem eam non particulari tribuit, sed universali.
Quare *duobus modis* videtur Averroes aberrasse. Tu vero si
melius fueris interpretatus, videbis clarius aberrasse Averroem,
nam hoc in loco Aristoteles exacte dixit. Namque si ejusmodi
universalis cum prædicato quod *universaliter* prædicatur, est
falsa semper, nullamque talem esse arti aptam, tenendum est.
Quare, si universalis ea ejecta est, etiam ea universalis cum
prædicato quod *particulariter prædicatur* ejicienda est, vel si vera
sit ? Non enim opponi potest illi, quod in arte ipsa non habet
locum ; præsertim quum in hoc loco omnis enunciatio conside-
rata in oppositione collocatur. Quinetiam neque usquequaque
nota *particularitatis* addita prædicato superflua est, neque falsam
reddit enunciationem. Dicentes enim, *omnis substantia quoddam
ens est,* vere dicimus ; atque si determinamus ita dicentes, non
etiam superflua erit ea additio. Dicentes enim *substantiam esse
ens,* verum dicimus, non quia ipsum ens, usquequaque inest
prædicato substantiæ, sed quia *pars* entis est, quæ de substantia prædicatur. Quod, ubi determinantes, significamus, non
inepte facimus et superflue ; monemus enim ita, ne per multa
vagetur audientis animus. Quamobrem in more est Aristoteli uti
hujusmodi genere loquendi, *cum ea nota addita prædicato.* Veluti

in primo De Moribus, 'Omnis ars,' inquit, ' et omnis doctrina atque actio, similiter et electio, bonum *quoddam* expetere videtur;' et in sexto, 'Divinæ hæ omnes,' inquit, 'unum *quoddam*, genusque *quodpiam* exceptum sumentes, de hoc, non de ente simpliciter, neque ut est ens, considerationes suas efficiunt.' Quamobrem et si nota *particularitatis* addita prædicato faciat enunciationem ineptam in oppositionibus ; non usquequaque tamen inutilis est, atque idcirco Aristoteles *de ea nihil locutus est*. Nam quoad oppositionem, de ea determinatum est—non esse recipiendam ; quo vero ad modum loquendi determinate—non esse rejiciendam putavit, *sed non rejiciens illam admisit*. Quod si de nota *universalitatis* addita prædicato, qua *superflua* est, locutus est in Prioribus Analyticis, hic vero *non* locutus est, nihil mirum est; hic enim, de oppositionibus enunciationum disputaturus, considerat eas enunciationes, quæ in eis clausuram (?) ponunt, quæ vero inesse non potest in oppositione, illa rejecta manet, *nec oportet amplius considerare et de rejecta*, an sit in ea *superfluitas*. In priore vero Priorum prohibetur *nota universalitatis in prædicato*, tum quia est impossibilis propositio, tum quia si esset vera, esset inutilis illi, qui facultatem quærit medii inveniendi ; quippe quod ei satis sit, simpliciter prædicatum referre.—His ita se habentibus, patet male dixisse Averroem de nota *particularitatis*, addita prædicato, tum quia non semper est superflua, tum quia superfluitas quæ spectabat ad universaliter prædicatum, transtulit ad particulariter prædicatum."—(*Castigationes*, &c., *in lib. De Interp.*, fol. 46.)

This is, on the whole, the most elaborate and acute criticism on this passage from Aristotle which I have met with ; and it quite triumphantly establishes against Averroes the particular quantification of the predicate. The way, too, in which Aristotle himself is made to uphold this view is somewhat ingenious: —that since, on the one hand, he does not reject it in theory, and on the other actually adopts it in practice, he must be held to have received and approved of the particular quantification of the predicate. Leo is very careful, while rejecting the interpretation of Averroes, not to oppose Aristotle; and I am half disposed to think that he was led into the adoption and defence of this particular quantification, as much through a determination to oppose Averroes when this was possible, without directly contradicting Aristotle, as from any previous insight into the question. His opposition has, however, in this case, led him into the partial adoption of a truth, which few of the commentators on Aristotle have at all perceived, but which he has so far very well stated and defended.

Jodocus Isenach,* or Justus Jodocus of Eisenach, was pro-

---

* Justus Jodocus Trutvetter Isenach, or as he was more commonly styled, Dr. Jodocus Isenach, was one of those devoted adherents to the ancient system of things, who formed so numerous a class in Germany at the beginning of the sixteenth century. Monastic scholars they were, for the most part, who were hostile to the Reformation, because they discerned in it a reaction against scholasticism, rather than because it menaced the unity of the Catholic Church. In the seats of learning, in Germany in particular, indeed, the battle of the Reformation was fought rather on the ground of letters than on that of religion; and when a religious plea was ostensibly urged in defence by those in authority, it was generally only as a mask under which they could more effectually attack their opponents. By these men the true faith was identified with an ignorance of letters and a knowledge of scholasticism. Those, therefore, who sought to disparage the latter, and to introduce the former, were necessarily heretics, and were persecuted as such. The fierceness of this persecution, indeed, combined with the obstinacy of those in power in clinging to a system now obsolete, determined a crisis in the struggle for improvement which had long been gradually going on, and hastened the complete reformation which soon followed. They would admit no innovation whatever in the existing system of instruction; they resolved not to modify in any particular their philosophical faith or teaching; and by thus blindly refusing to give up anything, lost all. To this class, as we have said, Isenach belonged; and to this it is probably to be attributed that so few particulars can now be gleaned of his history. Hardly any amount of individual genius was sufficient to save a single one of the vanquished in that warfare, from the oblivion into which all speedily fell. To those who were interested in the revival of letters, and the general progress of the Reformation, it became almost a duty to forget the names and reject the works of the abettors of ignorance and barbarism. Amidst the general enthusiasm which the new life had inspired, few were sufficiently interested in those who had sought to crush it at its birth, to redeem their names from forgetfulness, or hand down any record of whatever virtues they possessed, to posterity.

fessor of theology and philosophy at Erfurt during the latter part of the fifteenth and beginning of the sixteenth century; and if the slender accounts which I have been able to obtain of him be correct, was afterwards called to teach in the new uni-

Accordingly, with the exception of the very few particulars mentioned in the text, no specific biographical account of Isenach is to be obtained from any of the ordinary sources of information. The particulars there given are obtained from the Zedlerian Lexicon, which being one of the older encyclopædias, devotes six lines to his memory;—that being, I believe, the longest biography of Isenach to be found.

I have obtained, however, if not some additional particulars of his history, at least some materials for forming an estimate of his character, from another source, viz., the Letters of Luther, which contain some interesting references to him. Isenach may indeed be said to have been specially connected with the Reformation in Germany, since Luther himself was first his pupil, and afterwards, I was about to say, his murderer, but I ought rather to say, the cause of his death. Many grave accusations have been brought at different times against Luther, but none that I am aware of have ever laid this particular crime to his charge. He was notorious, indeed, for the summary manner in which he dealt with his opponents; but it was still not exactly in this literal sense that he was in the habit of destroying them. He was known to be a mighty man—mighty in the practical power which force of will and fiery enthusiasm bestow—mighty in the Scriptures— mighty, for that matter, in bodily strength; but it was, nevertheless, of the former kind of force rather than of the latter that he was used to avail himself in controversy; so that there would seem no just ground on which to urge such a serious charge. It is one, however, to which Luther himself in part pleads guilty. How far he really was so must be judged of from the sequel.

Luther was, as we have said, the pupil of Isenach. He was placed under his care, as it would appear, by his parents, in the year 1498, and continued for four years to attend his teaching at Erfurt. The two first of these were occupied with grammar, rhetoric, and other elementary studies. The third was devoted to logic; but he does not seem to have displayed any particular aptitude for the detail of that science, as he certainly does not afterwards recall the time thus spent with any particular satisfaction. After leaving Erfurt, Luther seems still to have kept up some communication, more or less direct, with Isenach. In particular, he seems to have been very urgent with him on the subject of scholasticism. Directly, by personal converse and by letter, and indirectly through his friends, Luther laboured earnestly and incessantly to modify his views as to the value of dialectic in theological training, and to abate his zeal in the interest of scholasticism. He was often, indeed, carried away by the strength of his feelings on these subjects; and what was intended as remonstrance became downright and stern denunciation. It was hardly to be supposed that Isenach

versity of Wittemberg. If this were the case, he must have
been a distinguished man, since none but the best men of the
time were called to occupy posts in that university. That he
really was so is confirmed by the manner in which he is referred

would be prepared to listen calmly to these denunciations of his favourite
studies. He regarded them indeed with the greatest grief and indigna-
tion,—feelings which deepened in proportion as Luther's zeal increased,
and were aggravated by the reflection, that this contemptuous rejection of
what he held most valuable proceeded from one of his own pupils. This
was indeed that "most unkindest cut of all," that went far to sever the
thread of his earthly life : so that Luther, on hearing of his death, writes
to a friend that he fears he is responsible for having hastened that event,—
so grievously had Isenach taken to heart his rash and profane condemna-
tion of the sacred writings of the schools ; in short, that he had died of his
(Luther's) contempt of scholasticism :—" Hac hora," says Luther, writing
to Spalatin, December 1519, " ex socero Lucæ [Cranach] pictoris audivi,
excessisse e vivis D. Doctorem Isenacensem Erfordiæ. Timeo et me causam
acceleratæ suæ mortis fuisse ; tantum ægritudinis fuit animo ejus ex meis,
ut dicitur, profanitatibus et temeritatibus, quibus scholasticam theologiam
doluit incredibiliter contemni. Dominus misereatur animæ illi. Amen."
—(*Luther's Briefe, Ed. De Wette*, vol. i. p. 373.)

How far this was likely to have been the case will be better seen from the
following extracts, which I translate from Luther's letters, on account of
their interest as illustrating the character of Luther, of the times, and of
Isenach.

The first extract is from a letter written in February 1616, to John
Lange, Prior of the Augustinians at Erfurt, inclosing a letter which he had
written to Isenach against the existing course of study. It is as follows :—

" I send you this my letter to the excellent D. Jodocus Isenach, full of
discussions against logic, philosophy, and theology,—that is to say, of blas-
phemies and maledictions against Aristotle, Porphyry, and the Sententiaries
—the accursed studies, to wit, of the age. For so it will be interpreted by
those who have vowed, not for five years, as the Pythagoreans, but constantly and to all eternity, to keep silent as the dead—to believe all things
—to be obedient listeners—and never, even in joke, to venture a skirmish,
or to breathe the slightest word against Aristotle and the Sentences. For
what will not be believed as truths by those who have such faith in Aristotle—who, himself the most calumnious of all calumniators, attributes to
others things so absurd, that an ass or a stone could not possibly hold their
peace at them ?

" See to it, therefore, that you carefully deliver these to that same excellent man, and be sure to smell out what judgment he or any of the others
may give concerning me in this matter, and let me know. For I desire
nothing more earnestly than to unmask that actor who has so befooled the

to by Luther, who speaks of him as "*princeps* dialecticorum nostra ætate." Isenach was the author of several works on various branches of philosophy; his logical treatises are, however, two, a larger and a smaller one. The former was en-

Church with his Greek guise, and to make his shame manifest to all, had I only leisure.

"But the greatest sorrow to me is, that I am compelled to see so many of our brother monks, endowed with excellent genius for all worthy studies, waste their lives and lose their labour amidst such filth as this; nor do the universities cease to condemn and burn good books, while at the same time they dictate, or rather dream out bad ones.

"I wish that Magister Usingen, and Isenach to boot, would abstain, in fact, contain themselves, for a while from these labours. My repositories are all filled [with writings] against their publications, which I am convinced are worse than useless; and all others would think as I do, were they not (as I have said) laid under an obligation of silence."—(Pp. 15, 16.)

The second extract is from a letter written in May 1518 to Spalatin, in which Luther gives him an account, after his return to Wittemberg, of the good reception which he met with from the Count Palatine at Heidelberg, and of his conferences with Isenach and Usingen. He says:—

"To the Erfurthians my theology is a dish of death in the pot—rewarmed; and Dr. Isenach made himself remarkable at Heidelberg, by prefixing to all my theses a black theta, [a mark of reprobation,] according also his written testimonial, that he considered me an ignoramus in logic, not to say divinity.

"I would have disputed likewise among them, [those of Erfurt, to wit, on his return from Heidelberg,] had not the Litany days* prevented. I had, however, a private conference with Doctor Isenach; and if I did nothing more, made him understand that he was unable to prove his own positions or to confute mine; nay, that their opinions, [or perhaps sentences, in which case the word will refer to those of Lombard,] were that beast which is said to devour itself. But the fable falls on deaf ears: they obstinately stick to their distinctions, confessing, howbeit, that these are established upon no authority, except what they call the dictate of natural reason, which in our eyes, who preach no other light than Christ Jesus— the true and only illumination—appears simply as a night of chaos.

"With Dr. Usingen I strove more than with any other (for he was my companion in the carriage) to persuade him of the truth. But I know not whether I made any way; I left him in thought and wonderment: so strong is prejudice when we have grown old in evil doctrines. But the minds of all the young were diametrically opposed to these veterans; and

* In the old universities there were certain holidays on which the prelections were put a stop to, and certain others on which not only the prelections, but also the academical disputations were intermitted. The days on which the Litany was used marked the latter.

titled, "*Summa Totius Logicæ*," and was printed at Erfurt in the year 1501. The latter, which seems to be an abridgment of the previous work, is entitled, "*Epitome seu Breviarium Dialecticæ.*" It is without any date, but was probably published not more

my hope is good, that as Christ passed to the Gentiles when rejected of the Jews, so now His true theology which these opinionative seniors repudiate, may be embraced by the young."—(Pp. 111, 112.)

The third extract is from another letter, written in the following month of the same year, to Spalatin, touching the value of dialectic in theological studies :—

"You ask, how far I think dialectic is useful to theology ; verily I do not see how it can be other than poison to a true divine. Grant that it may perhaps be useful as a sport or exercise for youthful minds, still in sacred letters, where simple faith and Divine illumination are to be awaited, the whole matter of the syllogism is to be left below, even as Abraham, when about to sacrifice, left the youths with the asses. And this, John Reuchlin, in the second book of his Cabbala, sufficiently confirms. For if any dialectic be necessary, that given by nature is enough, by which a man is led to compare one belief with another, and so to arrive at the truth. I have not unfrequently engaged in discussions with my friends as to the profit to be gained from this so sedulous study of philosophy and dialectic, and truly with one consent we have marvelled at, yea, bewailed over, the calamity of minds, finding in these studies no help, but rather a whole flood of hinderance.

"Finally, I have written to Doctor Isenach, the prince of dialecticians (as it seems) in this age, insisting most strongly on the same thing, which indeed cannot be denied, to wit, that dialectic cannot help theology, but rather hinders it, because the same grammatical terms are used in a widely different sense in theology and in logic. How, therefore, I say, can dialectic be of any use, when, after I enter on theology, the same term which in logic signified such a thing, I am compelled to reject, and to receive in another sense? And that I may not multiply words, take, for example, the following :—*Body*, in the tree of Porphyry, signifies a thing made up of *matter* and *form ;* but such body cannot belong to man, seeing that in the Scriptures our body signifies *matter* only, not also *form*,—as where it is said, ' Fear not them which kill the body, but are not able to kill the soul.' Farther, I instance the absurd statement, that an angel is neither rational nor irrational ; as also, that it is of no use to the Scriptures for a man to be called sensitive, rational, corporeal, animated ; and briefly, the whole of that arrangement of the tree of Porphyry, I have said, and still say, is more trivial than an old woman's fancy or a sick man's dream, and justly, therefore, is it called Porphyrean, (that is bloody,) from the Christian souls, to wit, which it has slain.

"The good man took it much to heart, and affirmed that my sophisms

than a year or two after the former, since its press-work manifestly identifies it with the earliest productions of the sixteenth

could not be credited even by myself. But these worthies are the bondmen of Aristotle and Porphyry, and consider not *what* is said, but simply *who* says it. Hence it comes that they are not able to understand a single chapter of Scripture, much less to render it.

" If, therefore, you accept my judgment, dialectic, of whatever use it be in other things, in sacred letters only does harm. I myself have observed the doctrines and rules of the scholastic theology, and have designedly endeavoured to treat the inspired writings and those of the Fathers of the Church according to them; but (may God condemn me if I lie) I recoiled in horror from the confusion, worse than that of Tartarus, [which this treatment caused.] But I will make the same attempt on you when we meet, and shall then detail, what you now briefly hear."—(Pp. 127, 128.)

These extracts are very characteristic of Luther—of his honesty—his thorough out-spokenness—his utter want of sympathy with the ancient barbarism, and his fiery zeal for its destruction. When we remember, however, that such deliverances as these were addressed to a man of whose character and history the only remaining record is, that he was a " lover of the scholastic theology;" and remember also, that they came with the bitter aggravation of having been given by one who had enjoyed the best opportunities of knowing the worth of the things he despised, since he had heard their value expounded by the ablest lips—the case certainly assumes a very grave aspect; and one can hardly wonder that Luther should have felt some misgivings as to his innocence in the matter. On the somewhat extravagant hypothesis, that such a catastrophe was possible to the abettors of scholasticism, there is here amply enough to explain a broken heart; and certainly the mildest jury that ever was empannelled could not have acquitted Luther of manslaughter.

The works of Isenach are now altogether forgotten. This smaller one on logic is the only one that I have ever seen. My copy is quite perfect, but contains no date, printer's name, or place of printing, nor has it catchwords or paging of any kind. Its title is curious, and (except the punctuation) is as follows :—

" Epitome seu Breviarium Dialecticæ, hoc est, disputatricis scientiæ. Iterum jam recusum; planiori siquidem, et præceptorum, et exemplorum filo.

" Per D[octorem] Judocum Issennachenum.

" Illitium Empturienti.

" Non sum, O Lector, Breviarium Romanum Moguntinum, aut id genus aliud, quo sacri Deo flamines supplicia fundunt; sed Logicæ, quo pueri prima ejus rudimenta haurire poterunt. Eme modo; non dices olim, quod Calcearius Romanus de Corvo suo,—Opera, et impensa periit."

Then follow a dozen of verses by Daripinus, Poet and Orator Laureate, which occupy the rest of the title-page.

century. This is the only work of Isenach's with which I am
acquainted; but the general knowledge and acuteness which it
displays, certainly go far to vindicate the justice of the title
which Luther bestows upon him; and to prove that he was not
only an accomplished logician, but what is far more rare, an
independent thinker in the science. It proves clearly, among
other things, that he was familiar with the use of a quantified
predicate; but what precise value he attached to it, or how far
he really employed it in the science, it is extremely difficult
from the work to determine. This difficulty arises mainly from
the circumstance, that this treatise being simply designed as an
introductory one, the longer, more novel, and abstruse discussions are left out of it, and we are referred for them to the
larger work. This is the case with those which relate to the
quantification of the predicate. When we come fairly upon
the subject, and hope to have it fully discussed, we are dis-
appointed in this, and get instead a quiet reference to the *opus
majus*, which to those who only possess the *opus minus*, and have
no access to the other, is provoking enough. Quite sufficient,
however, remains in this smaller work* to establish the fact,

* This work, though relatively less, is not absolutely small. It is a
quarto volume of some thickness, printed very closely, in the most con-
tracted style of the most contracting era of black-letter printing. In this
respect it is sometimes worse even than the work of Leo, three letters being
often deemed amply sufficient for a word of three syllables, and sometimes
for one of four. The text is, indeed, a perfect forest of large black-letter
contractions, overrun with a tangled underwood of smaller black-letter contractions in the shape of notes, and intersected continually with tables designed to render clearer, and sometimes to supersede the divisions of the text,
but which, owing to the ingenious interpenetration and general confusion
of their bracketting, are in themselves a new and independent source of
perplexity and bewilderment. This being the case, I will not undertake to
say that I am familiar in detail with every part of the work. I have looked
through the whole, read some parts carefully, and marked the passages
which seemed specially to bear upon the subject in hand. It is more than
probable, however, that some point of interest may have found its way into
some of those labyrinths of note or table which I have not yet perfectly
explored. The extracts here given illustrate clearly enough, however, the

that he was familiar with the quantification of the predicate, and that he employs it to some extent in the science. I shall accordingly extract from various parts of his work some of the passages which go to show this. These passages will necessarily be given out of their own connexion; and as I shall often be obliged to forego the comment they tempt, in order that this note may not be unduly extended, they will often be found to have no other relation to each other than their common reference to the principle in question. I shall first give some extracts from Isenach's exposition of *terms* and their *signs*, then from what he says of *propositions* and their *relations*, and finally select one or two passages from his comments on the *special rules of syllogism*.

In relation to *terms* he adopts the common division of *Categorematic*, and *Syncategorematic*,—the former including the subject and predicate of a proposition—the latter the various affections or modifications of these. On this second division he has the following passage, which I quote, both on account of its own precision, and for the sake of what is to follow :—

" Sincathegorema, quod per se et solitarie non est significativum alicujus rei vere vel imaginarie, sed junctum termino significativo et cathegorematico variat modum concipiendo rem significatam per ipsum, quod denotat ipsum accipi pro suo significato vel significatis aliquo more; puta universaliter, particulariter, singulariter, et cum iis; ut omnis, aliquis, iste, non. Nam dicendo *omnis*, nullam rem concipio vel intelligo; sed dicendo *omnis homo*, concipio vel intelligo hominem non simpliciter, sed universaliter *omnem*. Ita quoque dicendo *iste*, nihil addendo vel subintelligendo, nullam rem intelligo; sed quum dicitur *iste homo*, intelligo singulariter *hunc hominem* demonstra-

point in question, and are sufficient for the present purpose. I have some hope of being able to obtain the larger work of Isenach ; and should it prove of sufficient interest, will hereafter give a fuller account of his doctrine.

tum. Idcirco dicuntur hujusmodi signa nihil significare sed
duntaxat *con*significare. Unde nec grammatice, se solis possunt
reddere suppositum verbo; nec logice, esse extrema propositionis, sed solum *determinationes* et *modificationes eorundem*. Et
quia hujusmodi signa, ratione considerationis et habitudinis,
(puta, universalitationis, particularisationis, singularisationis,
distributionis, confusionis, et cum iis,) quam important circa ter-
minos sibi additos, mutant sensa propositionis et sæpius veri-
tatem vel falsitatem, idcirco logicus perquirit de ipsis hujusmodi
passiones."

This passage will serve to show his just appreciation of the
value of modifying marks as affixed to terms in restricting or
extending, or in general in rendering definite their meaning.
A little further on he says very significantly in relation to
these:—

" Illud vero quod ad copulam principalem est suppositum,
quocunque loco ponatur, est subjectum propositionis cum omni
quod ipsum determinat, dempto sincathegoremate, sumpto irrestricte sive non restricte; ut ' caput canis pilis intextum
habet homo decrepitæ ætatis:' ubi verbum '*habet*' pro suo formali
significato est copula, et idem pro suo materiali significato cum
hoc toto, ' *caput canis pilis intextum*,' quod ipsum determinat, est
prædicatum; subjectum vero est hoc totum, '*homo decrepitæ ætatis*.'
Simili modo judicandum est de illis : ' homo omni animali princi-
patur;' ' degeneres animos timor arguit;' ' velocibus alis mors
volat;' ' ignis et aer sunt elementa calida.' Additur, dempto
sincathegoremate sumpto irrestricte, *quum illud usu communi
logicorum non est pars subjecti vel prædicati*. Sincathegorema
autem sumi restrictive vel non restrictive stat in arbitrio uten-
tis. Fateor tamen, quod usu communi logicorum tunc sumitur restrictive quum ponitur a parte prædicati ; (ut ' Adam fuit
omnis homo,') vel inter partes subjecti diversorum casuum, et
determinat obliquum (ut ' conservans *omnem creaturam* est Deus.')
Irrestrictive vero sive non restrictive frequenter sumitur quum

ponitur in principio propositionis secundum veram construc-
tionem; ut ' omnis lapis est durus;' ' caput habet omnis homo;'
' verba dat omnis amans.'

" Scias tamen, quod sensus orationis variatur quum sumitur
restricte et irrestricte, verbi gratia, ' omnis homo est animal:'—

" Sumendo signum ' omnis.'
> *Restrictive* valet; ' aliquod existens, omnis homo est
> animal;' sic est falsa, quia nihil est dabile quod
> sit omnis homo.
> *Irrestricte* valet; ' quicquid est homo est animal:'
> vel sic, ' de quocunque verum est dicere quod
> sit homo, de eodem verum est dicere quod sit
> animal;' sic est vera."

I give a single extract from a long chapter on *signs,* (in which
Isenach often employs propositions with their predicates quantified,) mainly to illustrate his use of the terms *determinate* and
confused. At first, from his casual use of these terms in other
places, I thought that by the former he meant a term with a
mark of quantity, and by the latter one without such mark;
but it appears from his exposition and illustration that he
simply means by *confused* a universal subject, and by *determinate* a particular or individual subject. The following is the
passage :—

" *Confuse:* ita quod alterum extremorum denotatur ipsi convenire pro aliquo omnium suorum significatorum, hoc vel illo,
et nullo certo vel determinato; ut ' omnis homo habet caput,'
ubi denotatur quemlibet hominem habere caput, nec omnes aut
plures, unum, sed quemque suum. Et hic dicitur supponere
communiter, confuse, tamen disjunctim sive non collective.

" *Determinate:* ita quod alterum extremorum denotatur ipsi
convenire, inter omnia sua significata, pro aliquo certo et determinato, vel aliquibus certis et determinatis; ut, ' *caput habet
omnis homo ;*' ubi denotatur esse aliquid certum et determinatum

caput quod quilibet homo habeat. Hic dicitur supponere determinate." To illustrate this by an example which is given a
little below :—" ' Omnis homo non est omne animal,' ubi animal supponit confuse tantum : ' Anna non est omnis mulier,'
ubi *mulier* supponit determinate."

We pass to the consideration of *propositions.* Isenach's view
of the logical relation of a proposition is singularly just; and
his exposition of its scientific capabilities and significance is at
once comprehensive and exact. He explains in detail, that the
matter of a proposition is its terms, and that its true logical significance ever lies in the affections of these, and the manner in
which they are connected with each other. He divides the affections of propositions into those which belong to them considered
in themselves, and those which arise out of their relation to each
other. The former are of course *quality* and *quantity.* It is
with the last member of this division alone that we are now
concerned. In relation to it Isenach first gives the common
doctrine, with its four-fold division founded exclusively on the
quantity of the subject. He endeavours to explain the principle of his one-sided division, by saying, that the subject was
selected as being the more important part of the matter of a
proposition :—" Quantitas propositionis, hoc modo sumpta, penes
subjectum principale, vel partem principaliorem subjecti, dicitur quantitas propositionalis ; et ab ea propositio simpliciter denominatur aliqua denominatione ex jam dictis. Vocatur autem
hoc nomine propter hoc, quia subjectum est prima et principalis
pars materialis propositionis, atque principale fundamentum præ-
dicationis, de quo cetera enunciantur."

He then gives a statement of his own, as a supplement to the
common doctrine, founded on a far wider and juster consideration of terminal quantity. He asserts in effect, that the affection of quantity belongs to the *whole* matter of a proposition,
and not to *one of its parts alone,* as hitherto exclusively considered ; and that whether it fall on the subject or the predi-

cate it is equally of logical account. His statement is as follows:—

" *De quantitate terminali:* Solet etiam nonnunquam sumi quantitas propositionis penes quamquam partem materialem propositionis, (*i.e., quemlibet terminum cathegorematicum,*) non curando quocunque loco ponatur. In hunc modum :—

" Omnis propositio in qua ponitur (quocunque etiam loco) terminus cathegorematicus

1. *Singularis*, est universalis : ut ' ille asinus istius hominis est tardigradus.'

2. *Communis*

Distributus, est universalis : ut ' oculus cujusque hominis est aqueus ;' ' iste Deus est *omnis* Deus.'

Acceptus determinate, proprie est particularis : ut, 'hominis alter oculus est dexter.'

Acceptus confuse tantum, vel determinate reductive, est indefinita : ut 'Petrus est musicus.'"

He then goes on to make the following somewhat curious statement :—

" Hoc modo una propositio potest esse universalis, particularis, indefinita, et singularis ; ut patet de illa : ' alter oculus est cujusque hominis (vel istius hominis) dexter oculus.' Hæc quantitas vocatur terminalis, et ab ea non denominatur propositio quanta *simpliciter*, sed cum addito ; ut dicta propcsitio non denominatur simpliciter *universalis*, sed ratione illius termini hominis ; nec denominatur simpliciter *particularis*, sed ratione illius terminus oculus ; simpliciter vero denominatur *indefinita*, quia subjectum accipitur determinate reductive."

This he proceeds to apply to modal propositions, whose peculiarity, indeed, is logically considered, in the last resort, but an affection of the predicate.

The affections which belong to propositions considered in

their relation to each other are three—*opposition, equipollence*, and *conversion*. We shall extract without comment one or two sentences from what is said touching the first and last of these, and then pass on to the Syllogism. The following passages are from his discussions—the one of subalternate, the other of subcontrary opposition :—

"Terminus qui in subalternante stat confuse tantum respectu termini distributi in subalternata, non stet determinate respectu ejusdem termini distributi, sed accipiatur confuse tantum. . . . 'Omni tempore risibile est *omnis* homo ;' 'aliquo tempore risibile est *omnis* homo.' Sed subalterna prioris est ; 'aliquo tempore a risibile est omnis homo,' posito quod ly *a* faciat terminum risibile stare confuse tantum ; vel illa, 'aliquo tempore omnis homo est risibilis ;' vel ista, 'aliquo tempore risibile est homo.'. . .

"Si in una subcontrariarum ponitur aliqua universalitas, in altera omnia debent particularisari. Quare hoc non sunt subcontrariæ ; 'aliquo tempore risibile est omnis homo ;' 'aliquo tempore nullum risibile est omnis homo ;' sed subcontraria prioris est, 'aliquo tempore risibile non est omnis homo.'"

The last sentence on this subject is the following, which is at once significant and disappointing :—

"Oppositio non solum sumenda est penes quantitatem propositionalem, sumptam penes subjectum propositionis seu principaliorem ejus partem ; *sed penes quantitatem terminalem, quæ attenditur penes quamque partem materialem propositionis.* Potest itaque sumi oppositio, ex parte subjectorum, *prædicatorum*, et determinationum tam subjecti quam prædicati, atque etiam copularum. *Hoc est quod aliter dicitur.*"

The following is from his exposition of conversion :—

"Quod secunda, sive convertens, sequatur ad conversam, in bona consequentia, sic quod conversa non possit esse vera sine convertente : et propter hoc nihil debet universalisari in convertente quod non fuit universalisatum in conversa ; nec terminus stans in conversa confuse tantum respectu termini distributi debet in convertente stare determinate respectu ejusdem termini distributi, sed stet confuse tantum; vel terminus distributus in conversa non distribuatur in convertente. Cujus ratio est, quia in omni consequentia bona oportet caveri, ne arguatur a non distributo ad distributum, vel a termino stante confuse tantum ad eundem stantem determinate respectu ejusdem termini distributi.

" Propter defectum

Primi, non valet hæc conversio :

1. Omnis homo est animal ; ergo, omne animal est homo ; sed sic convertatur; quoddam animal est homo.

2. Nullus homo est *omne* animal; ergo, nullum animal est homo ; sed sic convertatur ; quoddam animal non est *omnis* homo.

3. Aliquod animal non est homo ; ergo, homo non est animal; sed sic convertatur ; quidam homo animal non est.

Secundi, non valet hæc conversio :

1. Cujuslibet hominis oculus est dexter; ergo, dexter oculus est oculus cujuslibet hominis ; sed sic convertatur ; ergo, dexter oculus est oculus alicujus hominis; vel sic, dexter oculus est cujuslibet hominis oculus.

2. Omni tempore risibile est *omnis* homo; ergo, homo est risibile omni tempore; sed sic convertatur ; ergo, homo est omni tempore risibile, vel sic ; ergo, homo est risibilis aliquo tempore.

" Volens itaque convertere aliquam propositionem, consideret diligenter, quæ sint ejus extrema, (puta subjectum et prædicatum,) atque habitudines logicas eorundem, (puta, suppositionem in genere, ampliationem, restrictionem, &c.,) *quas circa extrema exprimat, et subinde extrema transponat;* sic quod de subjecto fiat prædicatum ; et e diverso, constituendo aliam propositionem ejusdem qualitatis, in qua nihil universalisatur quod est particularisatum in priore, nec terminus aliquis stat determinate, respectu termini distributi, qui in priore, respectu ejusdem termini distributi, stabat confuse tantum. *Hæc enim conversio semper valet.*"

I quote the following passage mainly to show that Isenach saw clearly, what indeed he elsewhere more fully explains, that exclusive propositions distribute the predicate. It is the last passage in a chapter on exponibles :—

" ' *Tantum* homo est animal ' sic probatur : hoc prædicatum ' animal ' enunciatur de hoc subjecto ' homo,' et de *nullo alio ab eo,* (sive negatur ab omni alio,) et ita denotat per hoc signum *tantum.*—' Omnis homo est animal' sic probatur : hoc prædicatum 'animal' universaliter verificatur de hoc subjecto ' homo,' (sive convenit subjecto pro omni supposito,) et ita denotatur per hoc signum *omnis;* ergo, &c. *De quo alibi latius diximus. Hæc pro rudimentis puerorum sufficiant.*"

It will be seen that both in this passage, and in the closing one treating of opposition, reference is disappointingly made for fuller discussion of the matter to the other work.

Isenach's discussion of the syllogism is, in every respect, the most important part of his book. He gives an acute preliminary exposition touching the general rules of inference, some of which, as partially relevant to the question in hand, I had designed to quote. His discussion of figure, too, is curious and interesting, especially his doctrine in relation to the fourth. These points of interest must, however, give way to those which more immediately refer to the question of the predicate. These are the exceptions which he takes to the universal validity or necessity of the special rules of syllogism. He partially falsifies these by quantifying the predicate, as will be seen from the following passages :—

" 1. Ex puris affirmativis nihil sequitur formaliter in secunda figura.

" Cujus ratio est ; quia contingeret medium in neutra premissarum distribui aut singularisari. Nam prædicatum non distribuit in affirmativis (saltem de *communi forma* propositionum, in quibus *non ponuntur signa pregnantia.*) Si vero hoc caveretur, valeret argumentatio ; ut, ' omnis homo est *omne* animal ;' ' omne risibile est animal ;' ergo, ' omne risibile est homo.'

" 2. Secunda figura regulariter solum concludit negative.

" Nam, cum una premissarum debet regulariter esse negativa, oportet conclusionem esse negativam. Additur notanter, *regulariter,* quia, casu quo contingit *ambas premissas esse affirmativas,* sequitur etiam conclusio affirmativa ; *ut patet in priori exemplo.*

" 3. Minore existente negativa nihil sequitur formaliter, in prima et tertia figuris, directe concludendo.

" Quia contingeret argui a non distributo ad distributum. Nam, minore negativa, oportet majorem esse affirmativam, (quia ex puris negativis nihil sequitur,) et altera præmissarum negativa, oportet conclusionem esse negativam, et sic major extremitas, prædicatum majoris et conclusionis de communi forma propositionum, non distribueretur in majore sed in conclusione. Sed si hoc evitatur, (puta indirecte concludendo, vel quolibet aliter,) valet argumentatio ; ut, ' omnis asinus est animal ;' et

' nullus homo est asinus ;' ergo, ' aliquod animal non est homo,'
vel sic, ' nullus homo est *omne* animal.'

" 4. Tertia figura regulariter solum concludit particulariter.

" Nam aliter contingeret argui a non distributo ad distributum
ex parte minoris extremitatis.   Hæc enim distribueretur in conclusione universali in qua subjicitur, et non in minore affirmativa in qua prædicatur : ut est cernere exemplo, ' omnis homo
est animal ; et, omnis homo est substantia ; ergo, omnis substantia est animal.'   Verum si illud cavetur, quomodocunque
firma est argumentatio, ut hic: ' omnis lucidissimus planeta lucet;
omnis lucidissimus planeta est *omnis* sol ; ergo, omnis sol lucet.'

" 5. Majore particulari, nihil sequitur formaliter et syllogistice, in prima et secunda figuris, directe concludendo.

" Cujus ratio est, quantum ad primam figuram, quia contingeret medium in neutra præmissarum distribui vel singularisari.
Nam quum major sit particularis, medium quod in ea subjicitur,
non distribuitur ; et quum minor non posset esse negativa (ex
superiori regula) in qua medium prædicatur, nec in illa distribuitur, de communi forma propositionum, uti hoc claret exemplo.
' Animal est asinus ; et, omnis homo est animal ; ergo, omnis
homo est asinus.' " (Omitting his application of his rule to the
second, I pass on to his refutation of it in relation to the first
figure :) " Verum si hujusmodi *inconvenientia vitantur* (ut puta indirecte concludendo, vel quolibet aliter,) *valebunt argumentationes* ;
ut, ' lucidissimus planeta lucet ; et, omnis sol est *omnis* lucidissimus planeta ; ergo, sol lucet :' ' Animal currit ; et omnis homo
est *idem* animal ; ergo, homo currit.' "

It is here clearly stated, that if the syllogism be taken in its
regular form, as commonly considered, and as exclusively allowed by logicians, the rules are valid.   The reason of this is

explained by showing what logical vice would be committed if they were violated; but it is quite truly added, that if we can avoid committing this vice in any other way than by obeying the rules, the syllogism is good, and the rules, therefore, no longer hold. This Isenach shows can be done by quantifying the predicate. He accordingly falsifies the two first rules by a syllogism of the following form :—

> All A is all B.
> All C is B.   Therefore,
> All C is A.

He partially falsifies the third rule by a syllogism in the following form, in which the predicate is not quantified in the premises, but in the conclusion :—

> All B is A.
> No C is B.   Therefore,
> Some A is not C.   Or,
> Not any C is all A.

The fourth rule is falsified by a syllogism in the following form :—

> All B is A.
> All B is all C.   Therefore,
> All C is A.

And finally, the last rule is falsified to its first division by one in the following form, which, except that it is less definite in quantity, is much the same as the preceding one :—

> B is A.
> All C is all B.   Therefore,
> C is A.

Such is a brief outline of the doctrine of Isenach in relation to the quantification of the predicate. It is clear, even from this imperfect account, that he was familiar with its use, and, to some extent, appreciated its value. I am disposed, however, to think that he was far more familiar with its somewhat indiscriminate use in practice than conversant with its true scientific significance in principle. His insight into this does not appear to be great. Hence he often uses it capriciously, and without any particular end in view; and though, without doubt, he does occasionally employ it to simplify the working of the science, yet, after all, he does this very sparingly, and by no means to the extent we should expect from one apparently so familiar with its use. It is of course, however, as we have said, somewhat difficult to determine, upon such partial evidence, what precise value he did attach to the principle, since we are referred for this to discussions to which we have at present no access.

The last two writers whose names we have to quote in support of a quantified predicate are both much later than the preceding ones. We shall briefly quote from these the passages in which they partially allow in theory, or adopt in practice, such quantification.

The first is an Englishman, Joshua Oldfield, who, in his curiously discursive and ingenious " Essay towards the Improvement of Reason," which was published in London in the year 1707, touches, among other subjects, upon logic. Without professing to give anything in the shape of a regular system, he has some acute remarks on the syllogism, and among them the following, relative to the point in question :—

" The predicate of each enunciation is also supposed to be *universally* taken if denied, and *particularly*, when affirmed; so that in this latter case it ought to have a *note of universality added, if it be universally designed*, as it *may* be, in imagining a property, and *must* be, in giving a just definition, or a right description ; for these ought to be made universal when the proposition is converted, and such predicate put in the place of the subject.

" Now, when the affirmed predicate is thus universally taken, the argument will certainly admit of being otherwise formed than according to the usual allowed *moods* or *modes.*"—(P. 248.)

" Now, whereas it is commonly said, the enunciations must be so and so, (as in the technical words before mentioned,) and that there can be no more concluding moods in such respective figures, it must be understood to be so upon the forementioned suppositions as to the *quantity of the predicate;* for otherwise, where this is universally affirmed, there may be, *e. g.,* such a mode as ITALI in the first figure ; thus :—

I- ⎧Aliquod trilaterum est æquiangulum ;
TA- ⎨Omne triangulum est (omne) trilaterum ;
LI. ⎩Ergo, aliquod triangulum est æquiangulum.

In English, thus,—

I- ⎧Some three-sided figure has equal angles ;
TA- ⎨Every triangle is any three-sided figure ;
LI. ⎩Therefore, some triangle has equal angles."—(P. 250.)

These are the passages relative to the point in question which are to be found in Oldfield, who is the only English writer, so far as I know, by whom the quantification of the predicate is in any form allowed. It will be seen, however, from these extracts, how little he understood the principle which for the time he uses, since he even attributes to it none but a *material* cogency, and grants that the syllogisms commonly recognised by logicians are the only ones which are of formal, and thus of universal validity. It is also further manifest how limited was his view of its practical application ; since, both in its statement and illustration, he confines his attention exclusively to the case of universal quantification, and this is considered only in relation to affirmative propositions which contain a definition or description.

The last instance to be adduced of the partial use of a quantified predicate is that of Godfrey Ploucquet. He lived during the greater part of the last century, was for many years Professor in the University of Tübingen, and published many small, but acute, and often original, treatises in connexion with logic and philosophy. The only work of his, however, with which I am acquainted is that entitled " Fundamenta Philosophiæ Speculativæ," and published at Tübingen in the year 1759. In this work he employs the quantification of the predicate, in his treatment of propositions, to simplify their conversion. The following are the passages in which he does this, and they fully explain its use in his hands. I quote first, however, in order to render what follows intelligible, his own explanation of the peculiar symbols he employs :—

§ 34. " O præfixum denotat omnitudinem positive sumtam.

N præfixum denotat omnitudinem negative sumtam.

Q vel q. præfixa denotant particularitatem.

Duæ pluresve litteræ conjunctæ significant subjectum cum suis prædicatis. v. g. AB significat subjectum A cum prædicato B.

ABC significat subjectum A, cui inest prædicatum B, quod prædicatum B includit simul prædicatum C.

A—B denotat, A est B.

A > B denotat, A non est B.

N.A—B denotat, Nullum A est B.

A præfixum propositioni significat affirmationem universaliter sumtam.

I, affirmationem particulariter sumtam.

E, negationem universaliter sumtam.

O, negationem particulariter sumtam.

Cum seriei cuidam subjungitur signum, &c., denotatur series infinita, vel integra. Cum non subjungitur, denotatur series abrupta."

§ 36. " Sit primo, propositio universaliter affirmans, O.A—B. Hæc in generalibus et in symbolis spectata non infert hanc O.A est O.B sed O.A est q.B, § 24. Ubi vero notandum, quod particularitas nunquam intelligatur exclusiva."

§ 40. " Sit particulariter negans q.A > B.

Omne, quod est B, diversum est a quodam A. Ergo N.B est q.A.

Not. Operatio hæc vocari solet Conversio propositionum."

§ 41. "Apparet hinc, conversionem propositionum nihil aliud esse, quam transpositionem eorundem terminorum logice expressorum, nec quidquam in sensu ipso immutari. Si enim in sensu aliquid immutaretur, propositio non amplius esset hæc propositio. Ita nec ex particulari fit universale, nec ex universali fit particulare."

§ 43. "Sit propositio identica O.A—O.B: Hic A cum B identificatur, adeoque conversio fit O.B—O.A.

"Sint enim duæ series:

$$AB. \quad AB. \quad AB. \quad \&c.$$
$$CB. \quad CB. \quad CB. \quad \&c.$$

"Hic C non potest esse diversum ab A. Si enim B est idem cum A, tum B non potest inesse $\tau\tilde{\omega}$ A & $\tau\tilde{\omega}$ non - A, quia idem est idem.

"Cum usitatus loquendi modus non secum ferat hanc proponendi rationem: O.A est O.B, sed pro hac propositione substituatur O.A est B; convertendo dici potest q.B est A, modo attendatur ad id, quod particularitas comprehensiva et definita sit intelligenda, quæ justo modo extensa potest coincidere cum omnitudine. Si vero exacte loquendum sit, propositio O.A est B distingui debet ab hac O.A est O.B.

"Brevius: O.A est O.B. Si est O.B, præter B nihil aliud datur; adeoque O.B est O.A per conversionem.

"Vel sic: O.A est O.B; hoc est: Omne quod est in A tam ratione comprehensionis, quam extensionis, est quoque in B. A et B igitur nullo modo differunt, adeoque A est B, uti A est A."

§ 44. "Sit propositio particulariter affirmans q.A est B.

"Hic aut q.A est q.B, aut q.A est O.B.

"Priori casu patet, convertendo q.B fore q.A; posteriori autem, O.B esse q.A. Si enim quoddam A est quoddam B; patet ex hypothesi, nec ad omnia A, nec ad omnia B heic respici; adeoque seriem ita esse concipiendam

$$AB. \quad AB. \quad CB. \quad CB. \quad AD. \quad AD. \quad \&c.$$

" Ex intuitione manifestum est, A et B non semper conjungi, sed tam A quam B cum diversis signis connecti. Ergo q.A — B idem est cum q.B — A.

" Posteriori casu autem sequens apparet facies

$$\text{AB. AB. AB. &c.}$$
$$\text{AC. AD. AE. &c.}$$

" Ex hypothesi non datur B, quod non insit $\tau\tilde{\varphi}$ A; adeoque, OB — A, sed tantum quoddam A est cum B conjunctum. *e.g.*, Quidam homo est miles. Non datur miles, de quo non prædicari possit, quod sit homo, adeoque omnis miles est homo, sed tantum idea *cujusdam* hominis connectitur cum idea militis. Sed cum in expressione consueta quantitas prædicati non determinetur; utraque propositio facta conversione habebit subjectum particulare."

It will be seen from these extracts that Ploucquet competently understood the use of a quantified predicate in relation to propositions. Strangely enough, however, he makes no use of it in his treatment of syllogisms, where especially, or rather exclusively, its higher scientific value rises into view. With the exception of two short sentences, (if I remember aright, for I speak only from past reading,) he gives no intimation of its use in relation to syllogisms. These sentences are both notes. The first, which is appended as an exceptional provision to the rule, that from two particular propositions nothing follows, is this:—" Hic tantum agitur de expressione conclusionis consueta, ubi prædicato non addi solet signum quantitativum." The second, which is given at the end of his consideration of the third figure, and is to the effect that valid negative syllogisms may be obtained in it, is as follows:—" Si in propositionibus particulariter negantibus adjiciatur prædicato signum particularitatis; figura hæc procedit in omnibus modis supra recensitis."

This want of anything like a scientific application of the principle to the syllogism may indeed be said to be universal.

None of those to whom we have referred as having partially appreciated it, seem to have been at all aware of its value in relation to the forms of reasoning; but, after having applied it to some particular detail in the treatment of propositions, or at most to some exceptional case of syllogism, appear to have abandoned it altogether.

The promised historical evidence touching the previous partial appreciations of the new doctrine properly terminates here. I cannot, however, close this note without quoting a curious passage from a recent British writer, whose contributions to logical science have not met with the attention which their merit deserves. This writer is Mr. Thynne, who would probably have become better known, but for the comparatively humble form which he has chosen as the vehicle of his logical discussions. These discussions were published in the form of notes to Walker's *Compendium of Logic*, which has been for many years, and, for anything I know to the contrary, still is, the text-book of Trinity College, Dublin. These notes evince a careful study of logic, and an acute comprehension of the science, both in its general scope and in its particular detail; they show also an amount of independent thought in relation to the science, very rarely indeed to be met with in recent logical writings. The paragraph I am about to quote is really a very curious one, on account of its strange prophetic significance. It is given as a note to a passage in the text, in which the author, after giving the common statement that there are in all 64 moods, and that so many are *in*valid, adds, " *accordingly there are* 19 *concluding moods.*" The note is as follows :—

" (8) This, as logicians say, is gratuitously assumed. Sufficient has been said by our author to establish that all other modes than these 19 are inconclusive, but nothing has preceded to verify the conclusions in these modes. This may be done by the axioms, even more easily perhaps than by the famous rules of Aristotle; but in the application of the axioms the distinction of the premises and extremes into major and minor vanishes. If *all men* and *some animals* agree with a third, they agree with *each* other; and it is indifferent whether it be understood that all men are certain animals, or certain animals are all mankind. And it is certain, that if syllogistic reasoning had been thus viewed and followed up, it would be more readily brought into practice, or rather—as it is already, in the general practice of reasoning, thus treated, imperceptibly because enthymematically—it would receive less distinction of mode and figure; and consequently require less rule, and admit of simpler and readier, although not more ingenious, complete, or elegant verification than as at present treated."

This prophetic foresight, however, exercises no beneficial influence on Mr. Thynne's own treatment of the science. Logic certainly receives no simplification at his hands; on the contrary, the whole subject of mood and figure is made, if possible, still more intricate by the ingenious involution and evolution of detail which Mr. Thynne has introduced into its treatment. He therefore does not accept the doctrine he foreshadows. He may be said indeed to have explicitly rejected the quantification of the predicate; for he has propounded a theory of his own in relation to quantification, which is, to say the least of it, of the strangest kind. Mr. Thynne holds that *quantification is an affection of the copula.* This is a confusion so strange and complete, that were it advanced by a less able author, it might be rejected at once. Anything, however, which is seriously urged by so careful a student of logic as Mr. Thynne proves himself to be, is entitled to consideration, and if found to be erroneous, merits at least the courtesy of a refutation.

Mr. Thynne adverts to his doctrine in several of his notes; but the passage in which he most clearly propounds it is the following:—

" Such marks of quantity, although grammatically qualifying

the subject, do in sense qualify the copula; intimating the extent in which the agreement or disagreement of the terms is declared—that this extent is implied to be, either general or partial. ' Every man is an animal' implies that ' man is universally an animal:' ' No man is a stone,' that ' man—is universally not—a stone:' and ' some men are just' that ' man—is in part of the extension—just.' "

On this I would remark generally, that even supposing it to be correct, and that we may thus explain the quantity of the subject, still no account is given of the quantity of the predicate, which on the same principle ought also to be an affection of the copula, and to be represented accordingly in the same manner. Thus, to take the last of the above examples, since this is the only one which is given in the regular form, Mr. Thynne having in effect quantified the predicate in the others by the articles, —this is, " some man is just," which, says Mr. Thynne, is truly expressed thus, " man—is in part of the extension—just;" but whether is this part of the extension of man equal to *all* just or *some* just? This is a pertinent inquiry, for " *just*" is indefinite and must be formally limited or amplified in the same way as the subject. On Mr. Thynne's doctrine, therefore, two parts of extension must be expressed by the copula, in some such manner as the following: " Man—is in part of its extension—just —in part of its extension." All of this on the doctrine in question save *man* and *just* belongs to the copula; in short, Mr. Thynne maintains that the terms of a proposition are always taken *absolutely,* and that all modification of this absolute meaning belongs not to themselves but to the copula. The absurdity of such a doctrine will be better seen from an example in which the modification of the terms is of a more definite numerical kind than that usually found in the ordinary examples; for as *all* modification of the terms, that is, *everything* indicating the extent of the agreement or difference existing between them, belongs to the copula, then necessarily numerical modification of extent belongs to it also.   Take then the following proposition :—" ten horses are equal in strength to a hundred men." This expounded according to Mr. Thynne's doctrine will become the following :—" horse (taken absolutely)—is, considered under the relation of ten—equal to man (taken absolutely) considered under the relation of one hundred : or a part equal in extent to ten taken out of the whole concept horse—is equal in a given relation, that of strength, to wit, to a part equal to a hundred taken out of the whole concept man."   The former way of stating it is contradictory enough, and in the latter surely no one will seriously say that the true subject is the *whole concept horse*, and the true predicate the *whole concept man.*

This criticism would be in part inapplicable, did Mr. Thynne, with Aristotle and some of the older logicians, and indeed with the Compendium itself on which he comments,—did he hold, we say, with these, that the copula is included in the predicate. It is manifest, however, partly from his remarks, and abundantly from his practice, that he does not do so, but with logicians in general considers it simply as the bond of connexion between two terms, and in the last resort, therefore, always the substantive verb.

Mr. Thynne gives the following illustration in confirmation of his doctrine :—

" This is not the only respect in which a circumstance grammatically associated with the subject is logically associated with the copula.   In the proposition above, ' no man is a stone,' *no-man* is surely not the subject, for the declaration is intended to be made of man, and not of that which is not man : nor is the copula *is*, for the relation is intended to be one of disagreement. The negation therefore is here logically a modification of the copula, although grammatically of the subject."

If the principle was unfortunate, the illustration is certainly equally so.   " In the proposition, ' no man is a stone,' " says Mr. Thynne, " *no-man* is surely not the subject, for the declaration is intended to be made of man, and not of that which is not man." Now, what is the declaration made in the above proposition? It must surely be, " *is a stone*," which, says Mr. Thynne, is intended to be made of man, and not of that which is not man, but which I cannot but think notwithstanding is intended to be made of that which is *not man*, since it cannot be truly said that any stone is a man; and accordingly that *no-man* is the subject. Speaking generally, it may be said that in any negative proposition the negation may fall on the subject, on the predicate, or on the copula; but that on whatever member it falls, it becomes truly a part of that member; falling on the subject therefore in the proposition above, *no-man* is the true subject.

Let us look, however, for a moment more closely into the matter. A proposition is but the reflex in language of a judgment; a judgment is the product of a particular mental act. Now, the whole question is determined by ascertaining specifically *what that act is*. It is, in brief, one of *comparison*. Two things (terms of any kind) are compared together in order to ascertain whether they stand to each other in the relation of determining and determined, of whole and part; in a word, to discover what is the extent of their agreement or difference. Now, does this extent of agreement or difference belong to the objects which are compared together, or to the mind which compares them? Surely when two things are compared together, and found to stand to each other in the relation of part and whole, that affection of quantity belongs to the things, and not simply to the mind which perceives them. But on the theory in question the act of judgment is not only *cognitive*, but *creative;* it not only *perceives a relation*, but also *creates the relation which it perceives.* This involves a double confusion; a confusion in philosophy of the *perceiving mind* with the *things perceived*, of the *mental act* with its *object:* a confusion in logic of *quantity* with *quality*, of the *matter* with the *form* of a proposition, of things to be connected with the bond of their connexion. It is indeed an error so manifest, that we need not dwell upon its refutation, and one which could only have been committed by so able a logician as Mr. Thynne through great haste, or greater oversight.

We have thus the subject of quantification viewed in almost all the aspects in which it can possibly be considered. The common doctrine considers it in relation to the *subject*; Sir William Hamilton as it affects the *predicate*; Mr. Thynne maintains that it is an affection of the *copula*; while Mr. De Morgan (after Lambert) has elaborated a particular quantification of the *middle term*. This last scheme, however, as but a trivial and practically useless refinement on a doctrine universally held by logicians, may be thrown out of account. Mr. Thynne's notion, we have endeavoured to show, must, as the result of a strange confusion, be at once rejected. The subject and predicate, therefore, alone remain to be considered. The quantification of these terms, as the ultimate constituents of logical analysis, is, we need scarcely say, all-important. Through the working out of quantification in relation to the subject, the existing logic has attained to whatever of perfection of detail it can pretend to; through its working out in relation to the predicate, it will attain to the whole perfection of which, as a science, it is susceptible. The former is substantially the work of Aristotle; the latter is equally so that of Sir William Hamilton.

To sum up, then, the evidence we have gained: We have found, on the one hand, that the express quantification of the predicate has been rejected with singular uniformity throughout the entire history of the science. On the other hand, that it has been sometimes partially adopted in theory, and at other times in various ways applied in practice; only, however, to amend some particular detail of the science—it may be to simplify the process of conversion—it may be to modify, by a problematical exception, some particular rule of syllogism. But we have also seen, that its want has never been signalised as a fundamental defect in the original logical analysis;—a defect through which the science had been encumbered by unscientific supports—disfigured by unscientific additions—dwarfed by unscientific restrictions, and thus shorn of its true beauty of proportion and completeness; that it has never, therefore, been employed as a principle to reconstruct the whole edifice of the science, and by removing what was useless, rejecting what was false, and supplying what was wanting, to restore it to its perfect and harmonious beauty.

Despite, therefore, the evidence of partial perception which we have adduced, the original statement, " that the principle in its full scientific significance has been altogether overlooked by logicians," is vindicated.

No. II.

ON THE CATHOLIC DOCTRINE TOUCHING THE IMPLICIT QUANTIFICATION OF THE PREDICATE.

THOUGH logicians have with one consent rejected the *explicit*, they have, nevertheless, always held an *implicit* quantification of the predicate. This was indeed absolutely necessary to the existence and working of the science. For since all reasoning is in the last resort but the comparison of two terms with a third term,—but the perception of how far two terms mutually agree or disagree through the perception of how far they agree or disagree with a third,—it is obviously not only important but imperative that the extent of these terms themselves should be taken into account. This is, indeed, the very essence of the reasoning. Apart from this there can be no measurement of extent, and no conclusion of identity or difference of extent as the result of such measurement.

In other words, in any syllogism the process of the reasoning and the evidence of its validity is the same, and it is the following :—the middle term is the mean or measure ; in the first place, one extreme is compared with the middle term, and seen to agree with it *so far;* then the other extreme is compared with the middle, and also seen to agree with it *so far;* and thereupon this identity of agreement is affirmed. But, in either case, if I do not know the extent of the term compared, (cannot take it, that is, in some *definite* extent,) I cannot tell *how far* it agrees with the middle. Or, again, if I do not know the extent of the middle term, (cannot take it in some definite extent,) I cannot tell whether the term to be compared agrees with it in extent or not,—whether it is part, or whole, or none. The predicate notion, however, in every reasoning is one of these terms, and stands in one of these relations. It is, therefore, absolutely necessary, as we have said, to the validity of the reasoning, that it should have a *definite quantity;* and a definite quantity, accordingly, it always has had in the science. This quantity, however, instead of being left like that of the subject to reflect itself in language according to the whole extent of its possible variation as an element of formal thought, was made the subject of arbitrary legislation. Logical law enacted that the quantity of the predicate should always be held *particular* in affirmative propositions, and *universal* in negative ones. That logicians by this arbitrary and unjust enactment crippled their science,—crippled it too in a useless and preposterous manner—could be very easily shown. The natural scientific action of one of its parts was at once interfered with ; it could only work now under given artificial restrictions—restrictions which had not the slightest shadow of scientific warrant for their imposition. These restrictions are, indeed, not only artificial but capricious, for no reason whatever can be shown why one term of a relation of quantity should be made the subject of arbitrary legislation rather than another. It would have been just as wise and just as scientific to have laid down arbitrary rules for the quantity of the subject as for that of the predicate. Why not, it may be asked of the logicians, place the subject under the same restrictions, and enact, for instance, that its quantity shall always be held *universal* in affirmative propositions, and *particular* in negative ones?

The whole subject may be illustrated more fully in detail by the use of a figure which we have already partially employed. The subject and the predicate may be said to be the legs on which the syllogism stands. Its free progress, of course, depends on the natural unrestricted action of these members. Logicians have, however, crippled one of these—the predicate —by preventing such natural action. In order, however, that the syllogism might work at all after having been thus maimed, it became necessary to provide some support for the crippled limb. This, accordingly, was found, and in the shape of a body of special rules, a crutch which partially supplied the place of the natural support, was realised. Why did not the logicians, we ask, since they had thus endorsed the principle of such a procedure, destroy the natural action of the other limb also, and provide it with the same artificial support? They would thus have solved the problem, how far the syllogism could proceed when altogether deprived of the native strength of its own members, and supported on *two crutches* instead of one;—an ingenious experiment enough, certainly, but one which bears exactly the same relation to the natural development of the science, that racing in sacks does to the natural exercise of the limbs in walking.

This ingenious problem, however, the logicians have not attempted in its integrity. They have remained satisfied with its partial solution in relation to the predicate. The laws which they have laid down for the regulation of its quantity are, as we have said, two, viz. :—

1°. That in all affirmative propositions the quantity of the predicate is particular.

2°. That in all negative propositions the quantity of the predicate is universal.

On these two axioms, as they are commonly, but of course erroneously termed, the whole detail of the existing logic rests. They have determined its peculiar form and necessitated its special rules. These special rules may indeed be appropriately described as a body of provisions to secure that the predicate is always really taken according to the quantity assigned to it in the axioms. This will be at once manifest by an examination of the demonstrations of those special rules which are sometimes given in logical works. These demonstrations contain of course the reasons on which the rules rest, and these will be found in every case to arise from the necessities of the predicate in relation to its implied quantity. We quote the following in illustration from the Port Royal Logic, where all the special rules are briefly but adequately explained.

" RULES OF THE FIRST FIGURE.

" *The minor must be affirmative;*

" For, if it were negative, the major would be affirmative by the third general rule, and the conclusion negative by the fifth ; therefore the *greater term* would be taken *universally in the conclusion,* since it would be negative, and *particularly in the major;* for it is *its attribute* in this figure, and would be affirmative, thus violating the second rule, which forbids us to conclude from the particular to the general. This reason holds also in the third figure, where the greater term is also attribute in the major.

" *The major must be universal;*

" For, the minor being affirmative, by the preceding rule, the *middle term, which is its attribute, is taken particularly;* therefore it must be universal in the major, where it is subject, which renders this proposition universal; otherwise it will be taken *twice particularly,* contrary to the first general rule."—Pp. 189, 190.

" FIRST RULE OF THE SECOND FIGURE.

" *One of the two propositions must be negative, and consequently the conclusion also, by the sixth general rule;*

" For, if both propositions were affirmative, *the middle, which is here always attribute, would be taken twice particularly,* contrary to the first general rule."—P. 193.

The necessity of these special rules is manifest, for of those of the first figure, if the *former* were violated, a term which, as the predicate of an affirmative proposition, was *particular* in the major premise, would, as the predicate of a negative proposition, become *universal* in the conclusion; if the *latter* were violated, the middle term would, as predicate in the affirmative minor premise, be *particular* there, as well as in the major, and thus remain *undistributed*. The same reason holds in the first rule of the second figure. The other special rules are susceptible of a similar explanation, as may be readily tested, by taking them and the two axioms of quantity, and working out the relation of determination which exists between them. These axioms are thus, as we have said, operative through the whole detail of formal reasoning, as it stands in the existing logic. Rejecting the *explicit*, and accepting only the *implicit* quantification of the predicate, the question to be determined by logicians was, —how many of the possible forms of reasoning are valid without such explicit quantification ? The commonly accredited syllogisms were the result of this examination. The special rules which protect them were generalisations from the causes which rendered the rest invalid. Those which severally, according to their figure, obeyed the conditions of these rules, were alone accepted. These reasonings were declared, moreover, not only to embrace all the valid syllogisms which could be obtained under such restrictions, but also to exhaust all the possible forms allowed by the laws of thought. This is, indeed, one of the grounds expressly taken by Pacius in his rejection of a quantified predicate. He says, (at the close of the second of the extracts given from him earlier in the Appendix,) that the quantification of the predicate is of no use to the syllogism,—that it does not at all aid its validity; and gives a syllogism in Barbara of the first figure in illustration of his statement. The answer to this is easy. The express quantification of the predicate will not, of course, help the validity of those syllogisms which have been expressly constructed so as to be independent of its aid; and the cogency of which, therefore, is complete without such quantification. All the syllogisms of the existing logic are of this kind; and their validity, accordingly, is independent of any such expressed quantity. But this does not at all prove, on the one hand, that even these would not possess a higher formal completeness with the quantity of the predicate expressed; or on the other hand, that there may not be *other syllogisms* whose validity entirely depends on such expressed quantity. This is indeed the case; for on the one hand, everything of force in a formal science ought to be formally expressed; and on the other, *there are* a number of forms of reasoning guaranteed by the laws of thought, whose validity is not only contributed to, but *constituted by*, the expressed quantity of the predicate. Looked at therefore from the lower ground of the axioms of quantity, and the reasonings possible through them, the expressed quantity of the predicate is not absolutely necessary; but, regarded from the higher ground of the laws of thought, and their scientific development, this quantification is not only imperative, but indispensable.

These so-called axioms of quantity, it may be worth while to notice, are but corollaries from the laws laid down touching regular predication; for if the only lawful predication is that in which a genus is predicated of its species, since the genus is always of wider extent than its species, when so predicated it can only be taken in *some part* of its whole extent, that is say *particularly*. Again, if it be unlawful to affix marks of quantity to the predicate, we cannot deny *some part* of a genus of one of its species; and all negative propositions must therefore contain repugnant species or genera, which will accordingly be denied of each other in their *whole extent*. The rules for predication, and those for the quantity of the predicate, thus at bottom imply each other. It would perhaps be difficult to say which were cause and which effect; or rather, it would probably be nearer the truth to say, that they are both the result of the same defective analysis and want of scientific insight. Out of this original defect have arisen, as we have shown, the complexity, the restriction, and the disorder, of which the special rules, and the syllogisms they indorse, are at once the evidence and the result.

The simplicity of the reasoning process, contrasted with the complexity of the rules devised for its guidance and protection, could hardly, however, fail to arrest the attention of some of the many thinkers who have from time to time undertaken their exposition. They accordingly have, in various ways, betrayed their sense of the want of thorough scientific simplicity and completeness which these rules indicated: some, as we have seen, by falling upon stray syllogisms which violated the rules, but which were nevertheless quite valid, without, however, being able to offer any theoretic explanation of the fact: others, again, by simplifying the syllogistic law in theory, without being able to show how this theoretical simplification could be realised in actual practice. A curious instance of this latter kind occurs in the Logic of Caspar Wyss, which was published at Geneva (where he was for some time Professor) in the year 1669. He reduces all the rules of syllogism, both the *general* and the *special*, to the single one, *that every syllogism should have three and only three terms*. We subjoin his reduction of the special rules as a specimen of the way in which he accomplishes this :—

" *De Regulis specialibus Syllogismorum.*

" Regulæ speciales syllogismorum sequentes ponuntur a Philosophis : I^a. *Regula specialis* est : *In
prima figura, major debet esse universalis.* Unde hic
syllogismus non valet : Omnis homo non est in hac
urbe ; Tu es homo ; E. tu non es in hac urbe. Item :
Omne animal non est rationale ; Sed homo est animal ; E. homo non est rationalis.

" Verum contra hanc regulam dici potest, illam non esse universaliter veram ; si enim tollatur ambiguitas, et sint tantum
tres termini in syllogismo, syllogismi primæ figuræ, ex majori
particulari, sunt legitimi : v. g. Aliquod animal est rationale ;
Homo est animal ; E. homo est rationalis. Quare dicendum
est : syllogismos superius allatos esse vitiosos, quia in iis dantur
quatuor termini. In priore enim syllogismo, homo aliter sumitur in majore, quam in minore. In posteriore vero, animal
aliter sumitur in majore, quam in minore, ut patet attendenti.

" II^a. *Regula specialis* est : *In prima figura, minor
debet esse affirmata.* Unde hic syllogismus non valet :
Omnis asinus est animal ; Sed homo non est asinus ;
E. homo non est animal. Item : Omne rationale est
animal ; Solus homo est rationalis ; E. solus homo
est animal.

" Verum contra hanc regulam, dici potest, illam non esse universaliter veram, eo, quod dentur syllogismi primæ figuræ, ex
minore negata, qui sunt legitimi : v. g. Qui non credit in Christum damnabitur ; Sed reprobi non credunt in Christum ; E.
reprobi damnabuntur. Quare *dicendum* est, syllogismos primæ
figuræ, ex minore negata, esse legitimos, si sint tantum tres ter-

mini; esse vero vitiosos, si sint quatuor termini, ut patet in syllogismis superius allatis, in quibus sunt duo media, adeoque quatuor termini. Nam in priore, asinus est medium in majore, non asinus vero, est medium in minore. In posteriore vero syllogismo, rationale est medium in majore, non rationale vero, est medium in minore. *Adde,* quod in ejusmodi syllogismis, animal aliter sumatur in majore, quam in conclusione, ut patet attendenti.

" III^a. *Regula specialis* est : *In secunda figura, major debet esse universalis.*

" Verum contra hanc regulam dici potest, syllogismos secundæ figuræ ex majore particulari esse bonos, si sint tantum tres termini, non æquivoci; esse vero vitiosos, si sint quatuor termini, sicut diximus, de syllogismis primæ figuræ; adeoque hæc regula, est superflua.

" IV^a. *Regula specialis* est : *In secunda figura, altera præmissarum debet esse negans;* juxta illud vulgatum : ex puris affirmantibus, in secunda figura, nihil concluditur. Quare hic syllogismus non valet : Asinus est animal ; Sed homo est animal; E. homo est asinus. Item : Asinus habet aures ; Tu habes aures ; E. tu es asinus.

" Verum, contra hanc regulam dici potest, illam non esse universaliter veram, cum multi sint syllogismi recti, in secunda figura, ex puris affirmantibus : v. g. Omne rationale est risibile; Omnis homo est risibilis; E. omnis homo est rationalis. Item: Omne brutum est animal; Omnis asinus est animal; E. omnis asinus est brutum. Quare *dicendum* est, ex puris affirmantibus, in secunda figura recte concludi, si sint tantum tres termini;

male vero concludi, si sint quatuor termini, ut patet in syllogismis vitiosis superius allatis. In priore enim, animal aliter sumitur in majore quam in minore; in majore enim, sumitur pro animali contracto ad asinum, in minore vero, pro animali contracto ad hominem. In posteriore vero syllogismo, medium, scilicet aures, aliter sumitur in majore ac in minore. In majore enim, aures sumuntur pro auribus asininis; in minore vero, pro auribus humanis.

" V^a. *Regula specialis* est : *In tertia figura, minor debet esse affirmata.*

" Verum, contra hanc regulam dici potest, syllogismos tertiæ figuræ, ex minori negante, posse esse rectos, modo, non sint quatuor termini, et nullus terminus sit æquivocus, sicuti diximus de syllogismis primæ figuræ; atque adeo hæc regula est superflua.

" VI^a. *Regula specialis* est : *In tertia figura, conclusio debet esse particularis :* Unde hic syllogismus non valet : Omnis homo est rationalis ; Omnis homo est animal ; E. omne animal est rationale.

" Verum, contra hanc regulam dici potest, syllogismos tertiæ figuræ, conclusionem universalem habentes, esse rectos, modo, sint tantum tres termini non æquivoci. In syllogismo autem, superius allato, sunt quatuor termini, eo, quod animal aliter sumatur in conclusione, aliter vero in minore. Quod si, animal, in conclusione sumatur eodem modo ac in minore, scilicet pro animali identificato cum homine, conclusio erit vera, omne scilicet animal, identificatum cum homine, esse rationale; et sic, syllogismus erit rectus, ut patet attendenti.

" Ex his omnibus *patet:* omnes regulas syllogismorum, esse superfluas, hac unica excepta, *in syllogismo, debent esse tantum tres*

termini, non plures, nec pauciores; et per consequens, omnia sophis-
mata, ad unum posse revocari, scilicet ad sophisma ab æquivo-
catione." *Logica C. Wyssii.* Genevæ, 1669, pp. 318-321.

All that is here said touching the certainty of obtaining valid
syllogisms, if we only avoid having more than three terms, is
quite true; but the question arises, *how* are we, under the existing syllogistic forms, to avoid having more than three terms?
The answer is more simple than satisfactory. It is, by observing those very precautions which the special rules enjoin;—in
other words, by recalling in practice the code which had been
theoretically abolished. The reduction of the special rules is
so far just, but not a single step is thus taken towards relieving
the science in its practical working from the necessity which
imposed them. This could only have been done by the express
quantification of the predicate, without which, indeed, many of
the syllogisms given by Wyss in his reduction are formally
worthless, but of which he does not seem to have had a glimpse.

No. III.

ON FIGURE.

THE opinions which have been from time to time held by
logicians touching the nature and value of the Figures, (that is
to say, of the second and third,) seem to have been very fluc-
tuating, if not inconsistent and even contradictory. Some have
maintained their independence as separate forms of reasoning.
Others, again, and these are the great majority, have maintained, that whatever value they possess is reflected on them from
the first figure, and thus solely derived from their connexion

more or less direct with it. Of the former, some inconsequently retained the doctrine of *reduction*, and thus neutralised by a vicious practice their purer faith; a few, again, altogether rejected it; while Valla (abolishing the third) even proposes to reduce the moods of the first figure to those of the second. Then, again, with regard to the *different members* of the syllogism in these figures, opinions seem to have been almost equally divided. The great majority maintained that the syllogisms in these figures had a determinate *major* and *minor* premise, and consequently a single determinate conclusion. Others, again, could see no grounds sufficiently decisive on which to establish such certainty of premise, and held, as Apuleius and Valla, in certain cases, two conclusions. The former, however, while at one in their belief, are by no means unanimous as to the grounds on which they vindicate a determinate major and minor premise to these figures. They all agree, of course, that the major premise is that in which the *major term* is found. All the difficulty lay in discovering the major term; and the ways in which this was attempted to be done are, so far as I have met with them, of the most inconsequent and assumptive kind.

Sometimes the *major* term was held to be the predicate of the question, or rather the term occupying the predicate place in the question, that, to wit, touching which the doubt arises; for example, if it were inquired whether man were a stone, *stone* would on this doctrine be the major term. Sometimes, again, the major was held to be the term which was first enounced; and often enough a major term was conveniently postulated through the arbitrary assumption of a major premise. The methods, indeed, by which it has been attempted to vindicate determinate members to the syllogisms of these figures, all resolve themselves, in the last resort, to *a begging of the question*. This was generally done in one of two ways; either a determinate conclusion was begged in order to establish determinate premises, or determinate premises were begged in order to obtain a single determinate conclusion. I had intended to have gone into this whole question at some length historically, and for this purpose had marked a number of references in various logical writers; but though those are numerous and varied in character, I do not feel that I am by any means in possession of sufficient evidence to determine historically what the catholic doctrine in relation to the above points really was. I have accordingly thrown them aside, and must for the present leave the statement given in the body of the work as it stands.

One thing, however, is plain; that from the earliest to the latest times the procedure of the other figures was felt to be less direct, and their conclusion less authoritative than those of the first. To rectify this imperfection two processes have been devised. The first—that of *Reduction*—is of old date in the science, and is that usually practised by the logicians; the second —which may be termed that of *Exposition*—is comparatively new; for though anticipated in some of its details, it is substantially Kant's.* This process is that briefly expounded and applied in the text. These two processes have this much in common—that they accomplish their end by the transposition and conversion of propositions. In the former, however, the change made in the proposition is accomplished by formal conversion, in the latter by real inference. Of *reduction* we have already spoken in the Essay, and need not dwell upon it again here. With regard to the process of Kant, it is itself as tedious and involved as are the reasonings which it is employed to explicate. It is at best but a round-about way of accomplishing what perhaps there is no need for doing at all. The new doctrine, in-

---

* Kant first expounded this speculation of his in a tract published in 1762, and entitled, "*The false Subtilty of the Four Syllogistic Figures Demonstrated,*" (Die falsche Spitzfindigkeit der vier Syllogistischen Figuren erwiesen.) This is, I believe, republished with Kant's Logic, in the French translation of that work by M. Tissot.

deed, does away with the necessity or usefulness of any such process. On that doctrine this exposition is itself expounded, and this abolition of the figures itself abolished :—figure appears in its true character as an unessential variation of syllogistic form ; the several figures remain in their integrity with whatever of special value they ever possessed, while the essential form of the reasoning, when fully stated, is manifest through all the accidental positions of its constituent elements. The same reasoning may be given in either of these accidental varieties of position ; but since it obviously appears as essentially *one*, its cogency remains the same, and reduction and exposition are therefore equally vain and useless.

No. IV.

ON NOTATION.

THE notation employed in the text is that of one of the systems devised by Sir W. Hamilton, in order to represent to the eye the various possible forms of reasoning by distinctive symbols. It has all the virtues of a perfect notation. It is simple, distinctive,* perspicuous, and complete. It can represent *any*

---

* That it be *distinctive* is a virtue of first account in any system of logical notation; for to borrow the accredited signs of any other science is on every account to be avoided. I need scarcely say, therefore, how earnestly I unite with Mr. Mansell in deprecating " that mathematical method of exposition," which is, as he truly says, in relation to logic, " alike injurious to the science and repulsive to the learner."

The introduction of mathematical symbols and methods of working into logic is indeed, on every account, to be protested against by all who are interested in the welfare of the science. The rejection of these is the more to be insisted on, as well-meaning efforts still continue to be made to improve logic by mathematical treatment, if not indeed to afford it mathe-

relation of the terms, *any* order of the propositions, *any* extent
of quantity. The letters represent the terms, the points their
quantity, and the lines with the letters the propositions. The
letters express, by position to the eye, the relation which the
terms have in thought, the middle being placed between the extremes. The meaning of the *points* has been already explained;
the *colon* denotes *universal* quantity, " all;" the comma *particular* quantity, " some." Of the lines the shorter denote the premises, the longer the conclusion; the thick end denotes the
subject, the thin end the *predicate*. Thus the first syllogism given
in the table would read as follows :—

> All B is all A.
> All C is all B. Therefore,
> All C is all A.

Negative propositions are marked by crossing the copulative
line on which the negation falls, as shown in the *premises* of the
negative syllogisms given in the table. I may here notice that
the cross is absent from the lines of conclusion in these syllogisms by accident, and not by design. It was omitted in the
cutting of the type; and I must request the reader to be good
enough to supply it by the pen.

This system of notation will now probably be generally known
to logical students through the exposition of it given by Mr.

---

matical protection. With all such help, however, it can well afford to dis-
pense; if it could not—indeed, if this were not to it hindrance rather than
help—it would have no claim to rank as a separate science. The notion of
extending the sphere of mathematics so as to include logic, is as theoretically absurd as its realisation is practically impossible. To identify logic
with mathematics is to make the whole equal to its part: while to subordinate the former to the latter is to increase the marvel, by making the
whole less than its part. And those who, without attempting this, display
their skill by translating logical forms into mathematical language, accomplish a work just about as useful and praiseworthy as that " of the two
zealous, but thick-headed logicians—Herlinus and Dasypodius by name—
who rendered the first six books of Euclid into formal syllogisms." All
such endeavours possess the singular merit of making logic as repulsive as
possible, without doing the least service to mathematics.

Thomson in his "Outline of the Laws of Thought," where further details respecting it may be found. Mr. Thomson says, in introducing his explanation, that "many of the different elements of the notation are not new." With all respect for the statement of so careful and zealous a student of logic as Mr. Thomson, I must say I cannot but think that this is a mistake. I do not know, of course, what authority Mr. Thomson may have for his statement; but, with some general knowledge of most of the previous systems of logical notation which have been employed, I cannot recall any which anticipate the present, either in notion or detail; unless, indeed, the bare use of lines, though in a totally different manner, can be said to do so. I cannot think, however, that this is what Mr. Thomson refers to ; for the *linear notation* is a separate system, altogether distinct from the one in question.

I had intended to have introduced here fuller tables, running the positive and negative syllogisms through *all* the figures, as well as some specimens of other systems of notation which Sir William Hamilton has kindly placed at my disposal. I am not without hope, however, that Sir William will himself publish them in full before very long ; and I need scarcely say, therefore, how gladly I relinquish their partial introduction here. I know how earnestly all who are interested in logical science will unite with me in the hope that Sir William Hamilton's health and leisure may be such as to enable him to carry through the press at no distant interval some portion of his promised work.

NOTE BY SIR WILLIAM HAMILTON.

THE following note contains a summary of my more matured doctrine of the Syllogism, in so far as it is relative to the preceding Essay.

All *mediate* inference is one—that incorrectly called *Categorical*; for the *Conjunctive* and *Disjunctive* forms of *Hypothetical* reasoning are reducible to immediate inferences.

Mentally one, the Categorical Syllogism, according to its order of enouncement, is either *Analytic* or *Synthetic.* Analytic, if (what is inappropriately styled) the conclusion be expressed first, and (what are inappropriately styled) the premises be then stated as its reasons. Synthetic, if the premises precede, and, as it were, effectuate the conclusion. These general forms of the syllogism can with ease be distinguished by a competent notation; and every special variety in the one has its corresponding variety in the other.

Taking the syllogism under the *latter* form, (which, though perhaps less natural, has been alone cultivated by logicians, and to which, therefore, exclusively all logical nomenclature is relative,)—the syllogism is again divided into the *Unfigured* and the *Figured.*

The Unfigured Syllogism is that in which the terms compared do not stand to each other in the reciprocal relation of subject and predicate, being in the same proposition, either both subjects or both predicates. Here the dependency of Breadth and Depth, (Extension and Intension, Extension and Comprehension, &c.,) does not subsist, and the order, accordingly, of the premises is wholly arbitrary. This form has been overlooked by the logicians, though equally worthy of development as any other; in fact, it affords a key to the whole mystery of Syllogism. And what is curious, the canon by which this syllogism is regulated, (what may be called that of logical Analogy or Proportion,) has, for above five centuries, been commonly stated as the one principle of reasoning, whilst the form of reasoning itself, to which it properly applies, has never been generalized. This canon, which had been often erroneously, and never adequately enounced, in rules four, three, two, or one, is as follows :—*In as far as two notions*, (notions proper or individuals,) *either both agree, or one agreeing, the other does not, with a common third notion ; in so far, these notions do or do not agree with each other.*—The propositions of this syllogism in no-figure are marked in the scheme of pure logical notation by horizontal lines of uniform breadth.

In the Figured Syllogism, the terms compared are severally subject and predicate, consequently, in reference to each other, containing and contained in the counter wholes of Intension and Extension. Its canon is :—*What worse relation of subject and predicate subsists between either of two terms and a common third term, with which one, at least, is positively related ; that relation subsists between the two terms themselves.*—In the scheme of pure logical notation a horizontal tapering line marks this relation ; the subject standing at the broad, the predicate at the pointed end.

There are *three*, and only three, Figures—the same as those of Aristotle ; and in each of these we may distinguish the orders of Breadth and of Depth.

The *First* Figure emerges, when the middle term is subject of the one extreme and predicate of the other ; that is, when we pass from the one extreme to the other, through the middle, in the order whether of Extension or of Intension. In the notation of this Figure, we may of course arbitrarily make either of these orders to proceed from left to right, or from right to left ; that is, two arrangements are competent.—There is here, determinately, one direct and one indirect conclusion.

The *Second* Figure arises, when the middle term is the predicate of both extremes; the order of Breadth proceeding from middle to extremes, the order of Depth from extremes to middle.

The *Third* Figure is determined, when the middle term is the subject of both extremes; the order of Extension proceeding from extremes to middle, the order of Intension from middle to extremes.

In the Second and Third Figures there is thus only one arrangement possible in logical notation. And as Extension and Intension are here in equilibrium, there is no definite major and minor premise, and consequently no indirect, but two indifferent conclusions.—This is best marked by two crossing lines under the premises, each marking the extreme standing to the other as subject or as predicate.

Of course each Figure has its own canon, but these it is not here requisite to state. The First Figure, besides its more general canon, has also two more special,—one for Syllogisms in the order of Extension, and one for Syllogisms in the order of Intension. And what is remarkable, Aristotle's *Dictum de Omni*, &c., (in the Prior Analytics,) gives that for Extension, whilst his rule—*Prædicatum prædicati,* &c., (in the Categories,) affords that for Intension, although this last order of Syllogism was not developed by him or the logicians;—both inadequately.

In regard to the *notation of Quality* and *Quantity* in the syllogisms unfigured and figured:—Negation is marked by a perpendicular line, which may be applied to the copula, to the term, or to the quantification.—As to Quantity, (for there are subordinate distinctions,) it is sufficient here to state, that there is denoted—by the sign [، or ،] (for the quantity of one term ought to face the other), *some;*—by the sign [:], *all;*—by the sign [.], *a half;*—by the sign [؛ or ؛], *more than a half.* The last two are only of use to mark the *ultra-total* distribution of the middle term of a syllogism, between both the premises, as affording a certain inference, valid, but of little utility. This I once thought had been first generalized by me, but I have since found it fully stated and fairly appreciated by Lambert, to say nothing of Frommichen.

Above (p. 76) is a detail of my pure logical notation, as applicable to the thirty-six moods of the first figure. The order there is not, however, that which I have adopted. The following is my final arrangement, and within brackets is its correspondence with the numbers of that given above:—The moods are either A) *Balanced*, or B) *Unbalanced*. In the former class both *terms* and *propositions* are balanced, and it contains two moods—i; ii, [=i; ii.] In the latter class there are two subdivisions. For either, a) the *terms* are unbalanced,—iii, iv, [=xi, xii]; or, b) both the *terms* and *propositions* are unbalanced, —v, vi; vii, viii; ix, x; xi, xii, [=vii, viii; iii, iv; v, vi; ix, x.] The following equation applies to my table of moods given in Mr. Thomson's Laws of Thought:—i; ii; xi, xii; vii, viii; iii, iv; v, vi; ix, x.—The present arrangement is also more minutely determined by another principle, but this it is not here requisite to state.

If we apply the moods to any *matter* however abstract, say letters, there will emerge *forty-two* syllogisms; for the formal identity of the balanced moods will then be distinguished by a material difference. On the contrary, if we regard the mere *formal* equivalence of the moods, these will be reduced to *twenty-one* reasonings,—*seven affirmative*, and *fourteen negative*. Of the balanced moods, i and ii are converted each into itself; of the unbalanced, every odd, and the even number immediately following, are convertible; and in negatives, the first and second moods (*a, b*) of the corresponding syzygy or jugation, is reduced from or to the second and first moods (*b, a*) of its reciprocal.

There are no exceptions. The canon is thorough-going. Only it must be observed: that the doctrine is erroneous which teaches, that a universal negation is not a *worse* relation than a particular; and that the identity of a negative with an affirmative mood, is regulated exclusively by the identity in *quantity* of the two syzygies or antecedents. The Greeks, in looking to the conjugation of the premises alone, are more accurate than the Latins, who regard all the three propositions of a syllogism in the determination of a mood.

It is not to be forgotten, that as the correlation of the logical terms ought to be known only from the expression, (ex facie propositionis aut syllogismi,) for all other knowledge of the reciprocal dependence of notions is contingent, material, and extralogical; and as the employment of letters, following upon each other in alphabetical order, may naturally suggest a corresponding subordination in the concepts which they denote : I have adopted the signs C and Γ, which are each the third letter in its respective alphabet, for the extremes; and the sign M, for the middle term of the syllogism. The scheme is thus emancipated from all external associations, and otherwise left free in application. I also transpose the former symbols in the interconvertible moods; so that whereas in the one stand C M Γ, in the other stand Γ M C.

W. H.

ERRATA.

Supply brackets to the extracts given from Ploucquet at the foot of pages 22, 23.

Page 48, second line from bottom, *for* premiss, *read* premise.

„   73, line 17, note, *for* tracing, *read* touching.

„   85, line 20, *for* eisque, *read* ejusque.